ENHANCING LEADERSHIP EFFECTIVENESS

Strategies for Establishing and Maintaining
Effective Schools

Marvin Fairman
Leon McLean

Printed by
Cross Media
www.crossmediamgmt.com

HOW TO ORDER:

Single copies, as well as quantity discounts, are available and may be ordered through the Organizational Health web site:
www.organizationalhealth.com.

ISBN 0-9745557-0-3

"As superintendent, I have found the Organizational Health improvement process to truly be a gift I can give principals to impact their schools' climate. Marvin Fairman and Leon McLean have taken the research on school leadership and translated it into a practical model and course of action for building leadership capacity and school productivity. Fairman's intelligent and sensitive training and the data analysis he provides enable principals and teachers to develop insight and powerful leadership tools. The Organizational Health concepts lead to a common language for principals and teachers that facilitates discussion and collaboration on school improvement efforts."

---Richard A. Middleton, Ph.D., Superintendent, North East ISD, San Antonio, Texas

"Superintendents who are searching for practical strategies for improving student performance should incorporate these leadership concepts into the culture of their districts. Prior to accepting my last two superintendent positions, both Boards of Education knew of my commitment to the Organizational Health diagnostic and development processes. Furthermore, they knew that a precondition for my accepting the position was that the Board of Education would fund and support the Organizational Health improvement process.

The *Organizational Health Instrument* and associated improvement strategies provide a systematic process for building the leadership capacity of leadership teams throughout a school district. The use of this process will clearly enhance results and assist in creating a culture that capitalizes on the skills and abilities of all team members."

--Bob Moore, Superintendent,
Oklahoma City Public Schools

ACKNOWLEDGMENTS

We are indebted to key leaders who have studied, applied, and integrated our previous work into their organizations. Personal interactions with leaders during our Interpretation Conferences, Resource Team Conferences and Team Training Workshops have challenged us to continue to expand and refine our conceptual models. Special recognition goes to the following current and former superintendents and key central office personnel who were responsible for incorporating and/or maintaining our diagnostic and development strategies into their organizations and have used our services for a minimum of **seven years:**

- Mr. John Bailey, Superintendent, Glen Rose ISD, Glen Rose, Texas; Associate Superintendent, Grapevine-Colleyville ISD, Grapevine, Texas; Principal, Tomball ISD, Tomball, Texas

- Dr. Bill Borgers, Former Superintendent, Dickinson ISD, Dickinson, Texas

- Dr. James Boyle, Superintendent, Temple ISD, Temple, Texas; Deputy Superintendent, Tomball ISD, Tomball, Texas

- Dr. Rosland Bratcher, Assistant Superintendent, New Braunfels ISD, New Braunfels, Texas; Jr. High Principal, Conroe ISD, Conroe, Texas

- Dr. Rex Carr, Assistant Professor, Texas A & M at Commerce; Former Superintendent, Edmond Public Schools, Edmond, Oklahoma; Superintendent, Tomball ISD, Tomball, Texas; Deputy Superintendent, Richardson ISD, Richardson, Texas

- Dr. Elizabeth Clark, Deputy Superintendent, Katy ISD, Katy, Texas; Deputy Superintendent, Hallsville ISD, Hallsville, Texas

- Dr. Jerry Cook, Superintendent, Duncanville ISD, Duncanville, Texas; Superintendent, Castleberry ISD, Castleberry, Texas

- Dr. Debra Cron, Superintendent, Weatherford ISD, Weatherford, Texas; Associate Superintendent, Garland ISD, Garland, Texas

- Dr. John Fuller, Superintendent, Wylie ISD, Wylie, Texas

- Dr. Libby Gardner, Superintendent, Pflugerville ISD, Pflugerville, Texas; Deputy Superintendent, Conroe ISD; Assistant Superintendent for Secondary, Conroe ISD; High School Principal, Conroe ISD, Conroe, Texas

- Dr. Larry Groppel, Deputy Superintendent, Dallas ISD; Deputy Superintendent, Highland Park ISD; Deputy Superintendent, Grapevine-Colleyville ISD; Superintendent, Lancaster ISD

- Mrs. Lynn Hale, Superintendent, Galveston ISD, Galveston, Texas; Superintendent, Arlington ISD, Arlington, Texas; Superintendent, Deer Park ISD, Deer Park, Texas

- Dr. Linda Henrie, Deputy Superintendent, Mesquite ISD, Mesquite, Texas

- Dr. David Hicks, Superintendent, Deer Park ISD; Associate Superintendent, Deer Park ISD, Deer Park, Texas

- Dr. Jerry Hill, Superintendent, Community Consolidated School District # 146, Tinley Park, Illinois; Assistant Superintendent, Garland ISD, Garland, Texas

- Dr. John Horn, Management Consultant; Former Superintendent, Mesquite ISD, Mesquite, Texas

- Dr. Ron McLeod, Management Consultant; Former Superintendent, Clear Creek ISD, League City, Texas; Superintendent, El Paso ISD, El Paso, Texas

- Mr. John Miller, Deputy Superintendent, Humble ISD, Humble, Texas

- Dr. Richard Middleton, Superintendent, North East ISD, San Antonio, Texas

- Mr. Bob Moore, Superintendent, Oklahoma City Public Schools, Oklahoma City, Oklahoma; Superintendent, Mesa Valley County School District # 51, Grand Junction, Colorado; Superintendent and Associate Superintendent, Amarillo ISD, Amarillo, Texas

- Dr. Sandra Mossman, Superintendent, Clear Creek ISD, Deputy Superintendent, Clear Creek ISD, Assistant Superintendent, Clear Creek ISD, Cluster Director, Clear Creek ISD, High School Principal, Clear Creek ISD, League City, Texas

- Dr. Dan Neuenswander, Management Consultant; Former Superintendent, Ft. Scott Public Schools, Ft. Scott, Kansas; Superintendent of Lawrence Public Schools, Lawrence, Kansas

- Dr. Mike Say, Former Superintendent, Humble ISD, Humble, Texas

- Dr. Tim Sonnenburg, Superintendent, Barbers Hill ISD, Mont Belvieu, Texas; Superintendent, Denton ISD, Donton, Texas

- Dr. Herman Smith, Superintendent, Bryan ISD, Bryan, Texas; Superintendent, Greenville ISD, Greenville, Texas; Superintendent, Taylor ISD, Taylor, Texas; Associate Superintendent, Amarillo ISD, Amarillo, Texas

- Dr. Monte Sriver, Management Consultant; Former Superintendent, Carrollton-Farmers-Branch ISD, Carrollton, Texas

- Dr. Donald Stockton, Superintendent, Conroe ISD; Assistant Superintendent for Secondary, Conroe ISD; High School Principal, Conroe ISD; Jr. High Principal, Conroe ISD, Conroe, Texas

- Dr. Walt Swanson, Superintendent, Stillwater Public Schools, Stillwater, Oklahoma; Superintendent, Center School District, Kansas City, Missouri

- Dr. John Taylor, Director of Staff Development, Conroe ISD, Conroe, Texas

- Dr. James Terry, Superintendent, Mesquite ISD, Mesquite, Texas; and Deputy Superintendent, Mesquite ISD

- Dr. Alicia Thomas, Associate Superintendent, North East ISD, San Antonio, Texas

- Dr. James Thompson, Consultant, ESC Region XI; Former Superintendent, Grapevine-Colleyville ISD, Grapevine, Texas; and Superintendent, Blue Valley Public Schools, Stanley, Kansas

- Mr. John Widmier, Associate Superintendent, Humble ISD, Humble, Texas

- Dr. John Wilson, Management Consultant; Former Superintendent, Clear Creek ISD, League City, Texas; and Superintendent, Amarillo ISD, Amarillo, Texas

We are also indebted to many superintendents and key central office personnel who have used our diagnostic and development materials for fewer than seven years.

We must credit Jeff Fairman for his technical expertise as a general resource and specifically for preparing the Organizational Health Profiles and Scatter Plots presented in Chapter 8.

A special thanks is due to Mr. Bob Moore, his Administrative Team, and the Board of Education in Mesa Valley County School District # 51 in Mesa, Colorado, for granting permission to report the coded research data contained in Chapter 8.

We are privileged to acknowledge the paradigm shifting work of Paul Hersey and Kenneth Blanchard for their now famous Situational Leadership model. They have graciously given us permission to reproduce some of their most salient points from their publications. We highly recommend their publications as leadership development resources.

The work of Stephen Covey has also been an inspiration to us and a significant influence in developing our conceptual models. His dependence, independence, interdependence Maturity Continuum provided us with the framework for integrating those concepts with the Situational Leadership model. Further, his principle-centered approach for personal and organizational leadership influenced us to structure our work around six core leadership belief statements.

Both wisdom and prudence dictate that we highlight the acknowledgment that this publication would not have been accomplished without the encouragement, patience, and quiet devotion provided by our wives while their husbands were "in labor." Therefore, we give our thanks and our love to Mary Ann Fairman and Brenda McLean.

Marvin Fairman
Leon McLean

Foreword by Lawrence W. Lezotte

Creating and maintaining effective schools where all students master the intended curriculum is simple--it's just not easy. The same can probably be said of most organizational change efforts. They are easy to describe but difficult to execute and sustain over time. In all these situations, the monumental challenge is "change" itself.

Organizations and the people who work in them have this curious habit of finding comfortable ways of behaving, day in and day out. Once these habits are formed, it becomes a real challenge to get the organization and its people to leave these comfort zones and follow an unknown path to an unfamiliar place. Fortunately, some organizations find change easier to manage and maintain than others do. Wouldn't it be helpful to discover why this is so? *Enhancing Leadership Effectiveness* provides valuable insights as to why.

Like humans, organizations are more likely to be able to meet the challenges of change when they are "healthy." In *Enhancing Leadership Effectiveness*, Fairman and McLean do an excellent job of describing the critical dimensions of organizational health. They then use them as a fresh lens through which to view effective schools as well as their less-effective counterparts. Their research and writing help us to understand how and why some schools are able to manage the challenges of change and others are not.

Over the years, I have been privileged to serve as both an analyst and advocate for the Effective Schools Model of school reform. The Effective Schools Model is based on over 30 years of school improvement research that has yielded a set of characteristics commonly found in schools that are effective in teaching all children. They are so important and so prevalent among effective schools that they have come to be known as the Correlates of Effective Schools. These correlates provide the framework for evaluating a school's progress toward the "learning for all" mission. Fairman and McLean, through their research and writings on the Organizational Health Instrument, have made a valuable contribution to that framework by clarifying why the Correlates matter as much as they do.

Leadership has been described as taking followers to a place they have never been and are not sure they want to go. As the yield of a crop is dependent upon the quality of the soil, an individual's success in leading sustained and continuous school improvement will depend upon the overall health and well being of the organization. School and district leaders everywhere who are committed to creating learning organizations where all students master the intended curriculum should read this valuable work. Therefore, in the long run, only healthy organizations will be able to create and maintain places where all students succeed.

To use an agricultural metaphor, the yield of whatever crop is planted is going to be significantly influenced by the quality of the soil in which the crop is planted. Likewise, the short and long-term effectiveness of a school or district is going to be dependent on the basic health of the organization itself.

--Lawrence W. Lezotte, Ph. D., Educational Consultant
and Reseacher, Effective Schools Products, Ltd.

TABLE OF CONTENTS

INTRODUCTION

Information Age Realities

Today is a vastly different world from yesterday. Today, "The only thing constant is change." Because these changes are multi-dimensional, multi-directional, and increasing in velocity, our world is evolving faster and faster and becoming more interdependent than ever before in history. The Information Age has literally invaded every aspect of our lives with new technologies that allow us to span both time and space and bring us closer together in a worldwide marketplace. The constant and compounding rate of change poses enormous challenges for organizations and their leaders.

Economically, in the United States we have made a huge social wager that we will be able to sustain our high-cost living standard. We are betting on our ability to maintain productivity at a high growth rate. In fact, we are counting on that indefinitely, as evidenced by the fact that our retirement investments are inside massive capital funds that will remain viable only as long as the businesses that they back prosper. Business can only do so as long as they can continually find a supply of skilled and committed workers. Information technology companies already scour the globe searching for well-educated young people. However, it is obviously unwise to count on borrowing talent from other countries indefinitely; we need to increase our capacity to grow and develop our own.

The U.S. educational systems cannot fail to supply great numbers of well-educated young people prepared to support and participate in the worldwide economy, people who are self-directed problem-solvers, team players, and who have a solid technological foundation. We can no

1

longer afford the luxury of deeply educating only the academically elite. There are not enough of them. Increasing this capacity will necessitate learning environments where no one falls through the cracks. Everyone succeeds. Creating and sustaining such learning environments will require diverse leadership capacity at all levels throughout the system.

Fundamental Reform Rationale and Framework

Let's briefly juxtapose what we need with what we have. Many public school reformers contend that schools are organized to achieve the operational mission of compulsory attendance but optional learning. Larry Lezotte and other Effective Schools researchers have advocated for compulsory *Learning for all students—no matter what it takes* for three decades. Until there is an internal mandate for this new mission that dominates the agenda at the school level and causes the adoption of innovative systems and practices, there will continue to be external pressure to adapt and change precipitated by dissatisfied customers.

As the U.S. public education system expanded and evolved during the Industrial Age, it logically became separated and institutionalized into:

- vertical layers of grades within elementary, junior high, and senior high;

- vertical silos—special education, gifted education, vocational education, college preparatory, etc; and

- horizontal silos—discrete content in mathematics, science, language, etc.

Each layer and silo had its own knowledge base, standards, and student expectations; consequently, because of Industrial Age structures and expectations, teachers were handicapped in their efforts to integrate curricula. Administrators were also systemically stifled in any serious attempts at synthesizing teaching and learning because of the rigidity imposed by such external and internal structures.

The degree to which this mission—compulsory attendance but optional learning—and this organizational layered and siloed structure still exist can be expected to cause the public outside and innovative professionals inside to express and demonstrate their discontent and frustration. As reform efforts continue to fail to systemically increase student achievement, the level of discontent and frustration increases. Apparently, the gap between goals and results is in fact a chasm that cannot be bridged by simply tweaking the existing system.

Therefore, perhaps it is time to refocus reform efforts. It can be argued that many school reform efforts have not challenged fundamental assumptions and perceptions about the traditional system. The magnitude of structural and systemic change necessary to meet the crisis of confidence in many U.S. schools simply cannot be effected with ephemeral changes to behaviors and systems. The issues are far more fundamental than fights about phonics and whole language or block scheduling, etc.

Many critics contend that the goals of the traditional system that was institutionalized by 1920 were—and are—to keep children in school and to sort them into "heads and hands."

Schools were charged with the dual mission of:

- deeply educating the academically elite, the "heads" in college preparatory programs, and

- preparing the remaining students to be productive members, the "hands" of the Industrial Age workforce and society.

Certainly this Industrial Age educational model fulfilled the nation's needs and fueled our development as a world leader. Even though this model has served us well, the rate of socio-economic change has mandated a rethinking of the alignment between what knowledge and skills people will need to be successful in the new economy and what students are getting in many schools. Even though the Industrial Age has long passed, the educational model it engendered still dominates the mindset and structure of public educational organizations today. It has become increasingly and painfully apparent that there is a gap between what our educational system is producing and what the new economy of the Information Age demands. In fact, many now contend that the previous Industrial Age model that served us so well in the past now has become dysfunctional.

Commerce in the digital Information Age cannot afford the luxury of supporting a dysfunctional system. In fact, the global competition characteristic of a digital economy will demand competencies from all. The identification of those competencies will emerge from a gap analysis of what students are currently getting as compared with what they need to survive individually and for the U.S. economy to thrive collectively. In order to make the quantum leap changes necessary, underlying paradigms must be analyzed, challenged, and changed.

The health care industry is experiencing such a paradigm shift, as the emerging belief is that the nation would be better served through more emphasis on attaining and maintaining wellness rather than on treating illnesses. This represents a significant shift in mindset because treating an illness is "outside-in" whereas wellness is "inside-out." The transfer of the implications of this mindset to school and schooling is that teaching, like treating, is outside-in; learning, like wellness, is inside-out. To meet the challenges of the digital age, school leaders will have to transform schools from places of teaching to centers of learning.

Industrial Age classrooms must be transformed to Information Age learning environments focused on developing 21st Century student, teacher, and leader competencies. Basing these environments on the democratic principle of *learning-for-all* will require significant change in structures, systems, and strategies for many schools.

Consider the effects of the following juxtapositions between Industrial Age and Information Age paradigms. During the Industrial Age, teaching was focused on instructing large groups in curricula that was predetermined by the educational system to be age and developmentally appropriate and that would hopefully be available for future recall by students "just in case" that knowledge was needed. That focus was facilitated by the teacher's role as a gatekeeper of knowledge and access to information. Evaluation of student progress was characterized by competitive classroom environments in which individuals were measured against group norms on teacher or textbook tests of student retention of facts.

This system was governed by time as a constant—class periods, grading periods, nine-month years—and learning as the variable, as reported by grades and cumulative grade points.

The advent of the Information Age industries has highlighted the need for a very different set of job skills than those that are the inevitable product of Industrial Age educational paradigms. Necessary 21st Century competencies will include such abilities as:

- transferring knowledge to application by learning and applying problem-solving strategies to real world, unpredictable problems using advanced technologies,

- working collaboratively as a productive team member,

- researching and determining the validity and relevance of information, and

- sharing information through a variety of modes.

Creating such learning environments will require significant departures from Industrial Age systems and strategies. New learning environments will need to be team-oriented, kinetic, visually rooted, and structured to engage students in active rather than passive roles. Students will be involved in constructing their own learning and applying their skills in broad ranges of applications in productive, work-like atmospheres.

Teacher focus will shift from being gatekeepers of knowledge to being facilitators of student access to relevant information for "just-in-time" learning needed to solve real-world problems. Organizational systems and structures will have to undergo significant change to accommodate programs where learning is the constant and time is the variable, where performance and high expectations dictate standards rather than time, place, and pace.

Developing such student competencies will require training/retraining a teacher population that will be characterized by the abilities to:

- facilitate, enable, and manage student-centered learning environments,

- apply standards-based criteria for student learning expectations to performance-based, relevant learning opportunities,

- plan collaboratively across the curriculum in order to construct student-centered learning opportunities that reflect real world integration of problem-solving and communication environments, and

- interact with the larger environment and culture as entrepreneur and public relations agent to facilitate accomplishing student objectives.

Obviously, leadership will be a motherload variable in effecting such changes necessary to implement the shift from the Industrial Age to the Information Age paradigm.

Historical Overview of Leadership

What did leadership look like and how did it evolve both in theory and practice during the Industrial Age? Educational leadership was shaped by the Scientific Management movement and the military management system because educational policy makers and policy implementers—school administrators—came primarily from the business and military establishments. They were grounded both in philosophy and practice in this Industrial Age model with its characteristics of hierarchical centralization, specialized job functions, and standardized roles and relationships. Inherent in this system was that knowledge and power and the reward system were vested in top positions within the organization.

Although the Ohio State studies reinforced the high task leadership orientation, they also acknowledged the need for high consideration. That model remained essentially unchallenged for several decades. The work of Paul Hersey and Kenneth Blanchard *Management of Organizational Behavior: Utilizing Human Resources* challenged the paradigm that the most effective leaders were not necessarily high task and high relations.[1] The following section briefly summarizes their foundation for challenging the previous paradigm and for formulating their Situational Leadership model.

In 1945 the Bureau of Business Research at the Ohio State University began a series of studies to identify various dimensions of leadership behavior. In their initial study, they isolated twelve key leadership behaviors. In subsequent studies and through a series of factor analyses, they reduced the twelve key behaviors to four and later to just two key behaviors. The two key leadership behaviors that were isolated in their studies are still the major foundations for any theoretical examination of leadership. The two key leadership behaviors that were factored out and measured on the *Leader Behavior Description Questionnaire* were Initiating Structure and Consideration.

Initiating Structure refers to:

> Leaders' behaviors in delineating the relationship between themselves and members of the work group and in endeavoring to establish well-defined patterns of organization, channels of communication, and methods of procedure.

Their study, like Taylor's Scientific Management movement, recognizes that leaders by definition have followers and that much of the work of the organization is accomplished through the efforts of members of the organization. Effective leaders, therefore, are those individuals who can initiate structure and can get tasks accomplished through the efforts of other people. By examining leadership on a single continuum, individuals could be described as having a style on this important dimension ranging from low to high on initiating structure.

LOW   **INITIATING STRUCTURE**   HIGH

Figure 1: Initiating Structure Continuum

The importance of leadership behavior indicative of concern for individuals and their personal relations was highlighted during the Hawthorne studies by Mayo and reaffirmed and renamed in the Ohio State Studies as Consideration.

Consideration refers to:

> Leaders' behavior indicative of friendship, mutual trust, respect, and warmth in the relationship between themselves and members of their staff.

By examining leadership on a single continuum, individuals could also be described as having a style on this dimension ranging from low to high consideration.

LOW	**CONSIDERATION**	HIGH

Figure 2: Consideration Continuum

In studying leader behavior, the Ohio State staff concluded that Initiating Structure and Consideration were separate and distinct dimensions and that a high score on one dimension did not necessitate a low score on the other. Therefore, behavior of a leader could be described as a combination of the two dimensions. Thus, it was during these studies that leader behavior was first plotted on two separate axes rather than on a single continuum. By equally dividing the Initiating Structure and Consideration continuums into halves, a 4 X 4 cell was created. As identified in Figure 3, four different leadership styles were clearly identified.

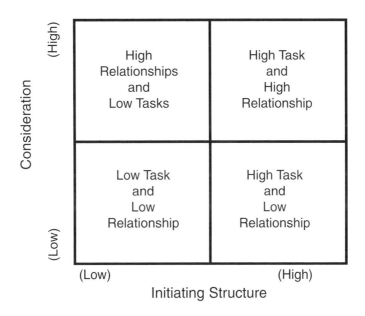

Figure 3: **Basic Leader Behavior Styles**

Approximately twenty years after the two-dimensional approach for examining leadership was established, Reddin expanded the concept to a three-dimensional one and entitled his work, *A 3-D Management Style Theory.* His work provided a major breakthrough and new perspective for examining leadership behavior.

His theoretical model introduced the belief that a leader's style may be effective or ineffective depending upon a given situation, thus challenging the earlier assumptions that the best style of leadership is **always** one which is high Initiating Structure (Tasks Behavior) and High Consideration (Relationship Behavior).

11

As illustrated in Figure 4, Reddin's 3-D management style suggests that the best management style is a function of finding the right combination of leadership styles for differing situations.

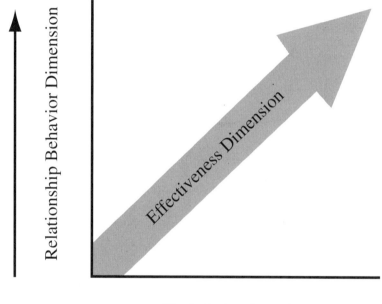

Figure 4: Reddin's Effectiveness Dimension

Situational Leadership, as the name implies, is based upon the belief that appropriate leadership styles will vary depending upon key situational variables. The keys to effective management are being able to diagnose the readiness levels of team members and other situational variables and to use appropriate leadership styles.

The keys to improving leadership effectiveness, according to Hersey and Blanchard, are:

- to help individuals improve their diagnostic skills, and

- to help individuals acquire new knowledge, to develop new attitudes, and to develop new skills that are prerequisites for utilizing each of the basic leadership styles.

Situational Leadership is a common-sense conceptual approach to help individuals improve their leadership effectiveness. Simply stated, Situational Leadership provides a framework for helping leaders match their leadership styles to readiness levels of their followers and other situational variables.

The theoretical framework for Hersey and Blanchard's model is built upon the early work of Taylor and the Scientific Management movement, Mayo's Human Relations movement, the Ohio State studies, and the more recent work of Fiedler and Reddin.

Building upon the early work of the Ohio State studies and Reddin's Effectiveness Dimension, Hersey and Blanchard developed their *Tri-Dimensional Leader Effectiveness Model.* The basic model includes the four basic cells which emphasize different levels of task and relationship

13

behaviors by the leader. The 4 X 4 cell in Figure 5 identifies the following four specific leadership styles:

- High Task and Low Relationship,
- High Task and High Relationship,
- High Relationship and Low Task, and
- Low Relationship and Low Task.

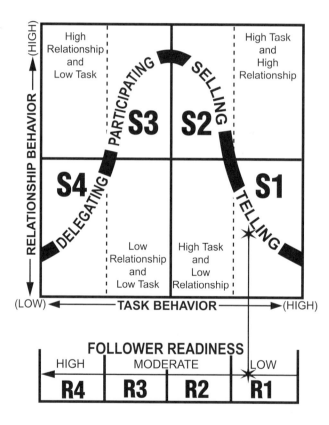

Figure 5: Situational Leadership Model

For ease of identification style categories have been labeled as cells S1 (Telling), S2 (Selling), S3 (Participating), and S4 (Delegating). Additional new components to their model include the readiness continuum and the prescription curve. According to their model, the appropriate leadership style is dependent upon the readiness level of the follower. If the leader diagnoses the readiness level as R1, the appropriate leadership style can be easily identified by drawing a perpendicular line from the readiness point to the prescription curve. The point of intersection on the curve identifies the appropriate leadership style.

The appropriate leadership styles for the corresponding readiness levels are listed in Figure 6.

Readiness Levels	Task/Relationships Behaviors	Styles
R1	High Task - Low Relations	Telling
R2	High Task - High Relations	Selling
R3	Low Task - High Relations	Participating
R4	Low Task - Low Relations	Delegating

Figure 6: Matching Readiness and Leadership Styles

According to this model, one of the first steps to improving leadership effectiveness is to realize that each team member has different readiness levels for different tasks. One of the keys is to improve the ability to accurately diagnose the readiness levels of members and to develop the appropriate skills for matching leadership styles with readiness levels. The readiness level of members is a function of both their ability and willingness to accomplish specific tasks.

According to Hersey and Blanchard, individuals' ability—or perception of their ability—to do a certain task will be a function of:

- their understanding of the specific job requirement,

- their job knowledge and skills, and

- their past job experience.

Likewise, their willingness to engage in a task and to complete the task is a function of:

- their willingness to take responsibility for the specific task,

- the degree to which the task will activate their achievement motivation, and

- their level of commitment to accomplishing the specific task.

As a leader, it is important to have or to gain objective information about your team members' ability and willingness to accomplish specific tasks. Making assumptions about an individual's ability without "checking it out" can lead to a major diagnostic error leading to an inappropriate leadership style. For example, an

16

individual's response or lack of response could lead one to conclude that the individual did not have the ability to accomplish the task (unable and unwilling) when in reality that person may have had the ability (able) but was unwilling. Thus, the readiness level was R3 rather than R1.

An individual's willingness to accomplish a task may or may not be related to ability. Willingness is related to the individual's motivation or commitment to accomplish the task. Active listening, asking clarifying questions, and paraphrasing can be helpful in gaining sound information about an individual's ability and willingness to accomplish a specific task.

Diagnosing an individual's willingness level may be more difficult to ascertain than ability. Unwillingness may be compounded by:

- competing forces for the individual's time and energy beyond the specific task or even beyond the work place,

- the belief that the leader should be the one to handle that task,

- a lack of trust and confidence in the leader, and

- group norms that discourage participation, etc.

As graphically shown in Figure 7, there should be a natural progression from low-to-high readiness depending upon a combination of the ability and willingness of the members to accomplish the tasks. It is understandable that individuals will range in readiness levels on different tasks from being unable and unwilling to able and willing.

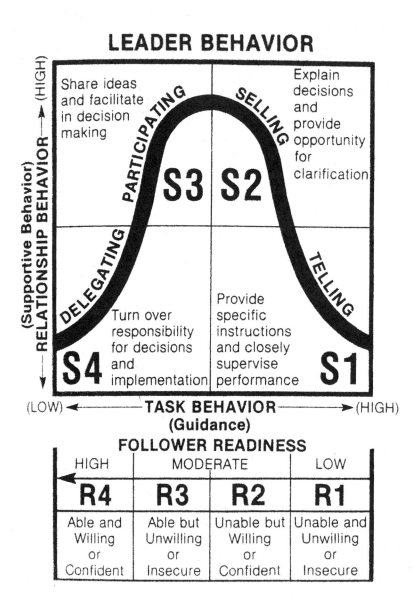

Figure 7: Readiness Levels and Leadership Styles

18

R1—Unable and Unwilling—Telling Style

People who are both unable and unwilling (R1) to take responsibility to do something are neither competent nor confident. In many cases, their unwillingness is a result of their insecurity regarding the specific task. Therefore, the most appropriate leadership style is a directive "telling" one that provides clear and specific directions. A "telling" style is characterized by the leader's defining roles and telling people what, how, when, and where to do various tasks. Too much supportive behavior with people at this readiness level may be seen as permissive, easy, and, most importantly, as rewarding poor performance. When individuals are unable and unwilling to accomplish the task, the leader needs to use high-task and low-relationship behaviors.

R2—Unable But Willing—Selling Style

People who are unable but willing (R2) to take responsibility are confident but lack the necessary skills. Thus, a "selling" style that provides both directive and supportive behavior is most appropriate. The directive behavior is important because of the lack of ability, and the supportive behavior will reinforce their willingness and enthusiasm. This style is called "selling" because most of the direction is still provided by the leader. The leader attempts to get the follower to "buy into" the desired behaviors through two way communication. Followers will usually support this decision if they understand the reason for the decision and if the leader provides help and direction. The leader's directive and supportive behaviors provide needed security.

R3—Able But Unwilling—Participating Style

People at this readiness level (R3) have the ability to do the job but are unwilling. Their unwillingness may stem from their lack of confidence or from a lack of motivation. In either case, the leader needs to emphasize two-way communication and active listening to encourage them to use their ability. A supportive, nondirective, participating style has the highest probability of being effective with individuals at this readiness level. This style is called participating because the leader and follower share in decision making, with the main role of the leader being facilitating and communicating.

R4—Able and Willing—Delegating Style

People at this readiness level (R4) are able and willing to accept responsibility. When leaders delegate tasks to individuals within this readiness level, they have confidence that they will make appropriate decisions consistent with the goals of the organization. Low-relationship and low-task behavior is appropriate because these individuals have psychological maturity and need little supportive behavior. When tasks are delegated to these individuals, psychological support is also provided via the delegation.

The work of Stephen Covey is consistent with the dependent and independent maturity levels of individuals as characterized by Hersey and Blanchard. However, his work extends the maturity continuum to include interdependent relationships for individuals and groups.[2] Furthermore, his work addresses the principle-centered base for effective leadership. Our conceptual models integrate and extend the work by Hersey and Blanchard and Covey. We have incorporated the dependent, independent, and interdependent growth continuum and the principle-centered leadership focus into the development of our conceptual models and leadership belief statements. Contemporary education reformers such as Larry Lezotte, Joel Barker, and William Daggett have also been challenging the Industrial Age model and calling for significant paradigm shifts to accommodate the dramatic changes inherent in the Information Age.

Conceptual Framework

What should be the leadership framework for this quantum leap transformation? Some critics have asserted that:

- fundamental change in education should be derived from schools adopting a business model,

- reform is the province of legislation by state and federal governments,

- change is prescribed best by universities,

- reform initiatives could be successfully driven by non-traditional top-down governance structures, such as mayors and industry CEOs assuming top school leadership responsibilities, and

- theoretical models based on publicly authorized, publicly funded, publicly accountable, but privately managed systems should be implemented.

The common thread for these reform efforts is the implicit assumption that public schools are incapable of fundamental change; therefore, they believe that the genesis of school reform must come from outside the system. However, given the less-than-inspiring track record of these outside interventions, it should be apparent that the best hope for systemic, sustained reform lies within the system itself, that fundamental reform is an "inside-out" model with decisions made by those closest to the point of implementation. Furthermore, those affected by the decisions should be appropriately involved in making those decisions.

Therefore, it is our belief that the best hope for systemic, sustained reform lies within the boundaries of educational systems. The challenge for educational leaders responsible for facilitating, supporting, and in some cases even mandating the reform efforts is to establish the system, the infrastructures, and support systems necessary for these fundamental changes. We believe that for this challenge to be effectively met, leaders must first be firmly committed to underlying principles that provide them with a solid conceptual foundation upon which to base and defend planned change efforts.

From over twenty years of Organizational Health research, developing and field-testing theoretical models, developing theory-to-practice materials, and consulting with learning organizations, we have identified six core principles that we believe should serve as the foundation for building the capacity of leaders throughout their organizations:

PRINCIPLE #1: A principle-centered mission provides purpose and true north direction.

Therefore, creating and sustaining the mission, vision, values, and purposes of the organization will create a framework from which quality decisions can evolve.

PRINCIPLE #2: Choices rather than circumstances control outcomes. People and organizations have the freedom to choose and are responsible for their choices.

Therefore, leaders should move organizational decisions as close to the point of implementation as possible consistent with the levels of competence and commitment of team members.

PRINCIPLE #3: Trust empowers others.

Therefore, leaders should capitalize on the expertise and commitment of individuals and teams by empowering them appropriately.

PRINCIPLE #4: The whole is greater than the sum of the parts.

Therefore, leaders should develop individuals and teams that have a high commitment to team efforts, which will require building a community of leaders who function interdependently as individuals and teams.

PRINCIPLE #5: Effective relationships require mutual benefit.

Therefore, leaders should encourage professional autonomy, which will promote interdependence both within and between teams.

PRINCIPLE #6: Quality Production (results) requires continual development of production capability.

Therefore, leaders should build feedback loops into the organization that will provide quality control and assurance strategies throughout the system. This process will assist leaders in aligning structures, systems, and strategies to ensure quality control and assurance throughout the organization.

If educational organizations are to improve—significantly and systemically improve—those who work inside them must take responsibility for focusing their efforts on building and sustaining commitment to a set of shared principles and beliefs throughout the organization. Such organizations will require developing leadership capacity throughout the organization because no individual can effectively and appropriately guide all decisions on all issues on all levels. Emphasizing this need for leadership capacity does not diminish the need for high quality leadership at the top of the organization; in fact, it mandates the need for a more sophisticated type of leadership.

Figure 8 presents a visual image of these six key leadership principles. This conceptual model shows that the mission, vision, and values for any educational organization is the focal and starting point for enhancing leadership and organizational effectiveness. The other key leadership principles of freedom and responsibility for decisions, empowerment through trust, synergy through team efforts, collaboration for mutual benefit, and balancing results and resources must be accomplished within the context of the principle-centered mission.

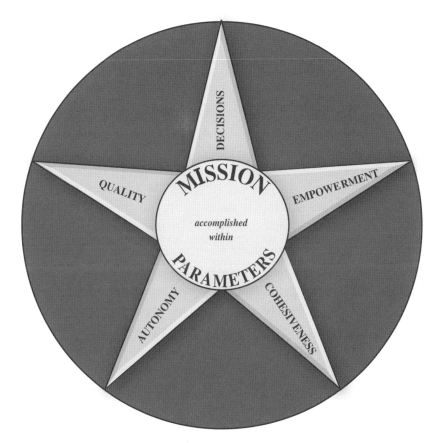

Figure 8:   Conceptual Model of the Six Key Leadership Principles and Belief Statements

In the following chapters, each of these key leadership principles will culminate in a leadership belief statement that is firmly anchored in sound theory and upon which effective practices can be based.

These six leadership beliefs are designed to provide the infrastructure to help leaders transform their organizations from inside out:

- We believe all decisions should be consistent with our mission and goals, should be data based, should be anchored in sound theory and practice, and should be focused on what is best for the short and long term interests of all students.

- We believe all decisions should be made at the most appropriate level in the organization and should be as close to the point of implementation as possible.

- We believe our behavior should promote and encourage empowerment throughout our organization.

- We believe we have an obligation to establish and maintain cohesive interdependent teams that have a high commitment to the organization's mission and goals.

- We believe our behavior should promote and encourage professional autonomy and inter-dependence for individuals throughout the organization.

- We believe that we have an obligation to build in quality control and quality assurance strategies throughout the organization.

CHAPTER 1

ESTABLISHING THE PARAMETERS AND THE FOCUS FOR QUALITY

Such inside-out change as presented in the Introduction can be best implemented in educational organizations that develop and maintain a results-oriented, quality-based focus on *learning for all—whatever it takes.*   Effective leaders need to collaboratively establish a set of leadership beliefs that help support and reinforce quality decisions throughout their organizations.

The following principle and belief statement are designed to help leaders establish those parameters for all members within their sphere of influence:

PRINCIPLE: A principle-centered mission provides purpose and true north direction. Based on this principle:

LEADERSHIP BELIEF #1

> **We believe all decisions should be consistent with our mission and goals, should be data based, should be anchored in sound theory and practice, and should be focused on what is best for the short and long term interests of all students.**

Adopting this leadership belief statement or a modified version of it may trigger the necessity of revisiting and revising the mission statement. It has been our experience that frequently when key leaders examine this belief statement, they typically say, "It sounds great!   But . . . but what is our mission statement?"

When leaders use the mission and the goals of their unit as parameters for decisions, it lets team members know that the mission and goals are important and should help drive the decision-making process. These concepts should assist leaders in improving the quality of decision-making by providing a standard for "measuring a quality decision." Furthermore, this belief statement will highlight:

- Using the **mission statement and goals** as filters for decision-making:

    o   reinforces the purpose and value of the mission statement and goals,

    o   identifies decisions that cannot withstand the test,

    o   provides an alignment check for the mission statement and helps keep it dynamic by testing it against the day-to-day operations, and

    o   serves as a feedback loop for goal accomplishment.

- Using **data** as an important filter for decision-making:
  o reinforces the relevance of data,
  o raises the level of dialogue from a "I feel" or "I think" to a discussion about data-based information,
  o encourages results-oriented thinking, and
  o promotes accountability and responsibility throughout the school or other administrative unit.

- Using the statement **anchored in sound theory and practice:**
  o highlights the professional role of educators,
  o reinforces professional accountability and responsibility,
  o requires principals and other key leaders to stay current, and
  o provides a filter for testing creative ideas.

- Using the statement **what is best for both the short and long-range benefit of all students:**
  o focuses on our real purpose by establishing parameters for a healthy and productive discussion,
  o reinforces the use of data and sound theory and practice in determining what is best for students, and

o highlights the criterion that professional decisions should be based on the needs of students—*whatever it takes*—not on what would be easiest or most convenient.

A leadership and organizational commitment to Leadership Belief #1 provides an operational system for **keeping the organization focused on its real purpose.** For example, when individuals internal or external to the unit want the leader to deviate from an existing practice, they know their proposal will need to be tested against this operational system.

Therefore, when individuals bring their idea forward, they will have "done their homework" prior to making a request. Consequently, the quality of the conversation will be at a higher level, and the quality of the decision should be enhanced. It has been our experience that leaders and team members throughout educational systems can quickly buy into and start using Leadership Belief #1 as a way to improve the quality of decisions throughout their organizations.

Based on our premise, leadership in 21st Century organizations should be an inside-out process where every leader focuses on establishing a culture where many people can develop and exercise leadership skills throughout the organization.

Therefore, a commitment to Leadership Belief #1 requires leaders to clarify and build consensus for the organization's **mission, vision,** and **values:**

- **Mission:** Why do we exist? What is our purpose? What stakeholder needs will we target, etc?

- **Vision:** What do we want to become? Where are we going? What are our short and long-range benchmarks, etc?

  Mission and vision define the "ends" and need to be clarified, reviewed, and renewed to ensure that the organization is moving in the right direction.

- **Values:** How will we behave and treat our stakeholders and each other? What will be our decision-making strategies? How will our actions be guided, etc?

  Values are the "means" by which the mission is implemented. Values provide the motivation and guidelines for action.

In fact, effective leaders have no choice but to clarify mission, vision, and values because it is impossible to exercise leadership where there is no perceived common ground. Shared values are necessary for collaborative, interdependent action.

The ability to forge this consensus is particularly critical today when unfortunately the bedrock for building values— the family and the community—is disintegrating in contemporary society. With diminished support for children in the nuclear and extended family, the church, and the neighborhood, they are increasingly seeking security from other sources including dysfunctional gang communities.

Likewise, without the cohesiveness that emerges from shared beliefs and values, the internal fragmentation, divisiveness, and competition will hinder organizations from accomplishing worthy purposes.

In order for leaders to be effective leaders, they have a responsibility for ensuring that all members of their teams are working and making decisions consistent with established values that are consistent with the mission and vision of their organization. Effective leaders are also skillful in helping team members formalize a set of goals and implementation strategies that build upon and are consistent with the mission and vision statements.

There are many effective strategies for involving members in the development of these mission, vision, and values statements; however, the identification and development of these strategies are beyond the scope of this chapter. The purpose for this chapter is to highlight the importance of having these key parameters in place and to use them to improve the overall effectiveness of the organization.

As depicted in Figure 8 on page 25, Leadership Belief #1 serves as the principle-centered core for the other five leadership belief statements. These six leadership beliefs are designed to provide the infrastructure to help leaders transform their organizations from inside-out.

CHAPTER 2

MAKING DECISIONS CLOSE TO THE POINT OF IMPLEMENTATION

Effective leaders are responsible for ensuring that quality decisions are made throughout the organization. By definition, quality decisions will be consistent with the mission and parameters as established in Leadership Belief #1. The effectiveness of organizations is impacted by the degree to which they have an effective and consistent method of responding to internal and external problems, issues, and concerns. The image and the reputation of organizations reflect the quality of their decisions.

Leaders are inundated with problems, issues, or concerns from internal and external sources. How do they determine if they or someone else should be involved or responsible for these decisions?

More specifically, how do they determine if they should:

- independently make the decision,
- seek input from others before making the decision,
- involve others in a collaborative decision,
- delegate the decision to an appropriate individual or team, or
- serve as an ambassador for interdependent teams?

In addition to who should make decisions, leaders also need to be sure that:

- their organizations have a process for keeping members impacted by the decision involved in and/or informed of the decision, and that

- someone is accountable or responsible for the decision.

The decision-making strategies that leaders use should depend upon the degree to which those closest to the decision point have the knowledge, skills, commitment, and time to resolve the issues.

As depicted in Figure 2.1 on page 36, leaders have access to seven basic decision-making strategies ranging from the leader serving as **arbitrator** to **ambassador.** These strategies are used for the day-to-day operations as well as proactive decisions regarding long-range planning.

Leaders need to know members of their teams so well that they will understand where individuals and teams are on the *dependent — independent — interdependent* continuum for a given activity. Since only independent individuals have the capacity to function interdependently, it is the leader's responsibility to provide the environment that fosters growth from dependence to independence.

The growth-point on the continuum provides a frame of reference for the leader and team members for determining the most appropriate decision-making strategy:

- When individuals and teams are *dependent* on the leader because of their lack of knowledge or experiences, then the leader needs to serve as an **arbitrator** or **negotiator** to resolve issues and to provide the necessary support.

- When individuals and teams are moving toward *independence* and need assistance from the leader as **mediator** or **facilitator,** the leaders need to provide the assistance and will purposefully help individuals or groups gain confidence and more independence.

- When individuals and independent teams are competent and committed to moving toward *interdependence,* the leader appropriately serves as a **delegator** and a resource person for their empowerment. When teams desire to collaborate interdependently, the leader appropriately serves as their **ambassador.**

The level of the *leadership capacity* or *leadership density* increases as individuals and teams move from dependence, to independence, to interdependence. Effective leaders invest time, energy, and money in the development of members of leadership teams, team leaders, and individuals throughout the organization.

From the leadership perspective it is important for leaders to understand that the decision-making strategies they use have both short and long term ramifications. Their attitude toward individuals and teams — or their team members' perceptions of their attitude — has a significant impact upon their success as leaders.

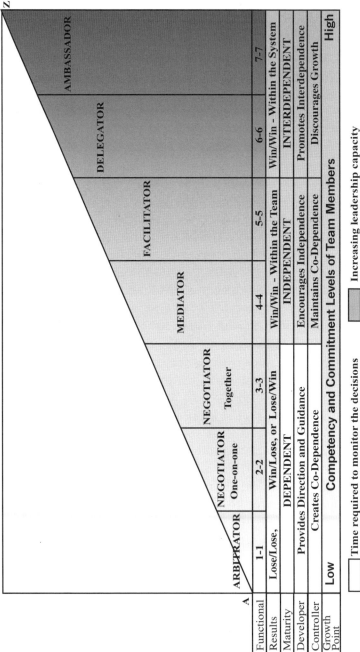

Figure 2.1: Decision-making Model

As depicted in Figure 2.1, leaders with a *developer attitude* are perceived as:

- providing the necessary support for individuals and teams when making **arbitration** and **negotiation** decisions,

- promoting and encouraging individuals and teams to become more independent and responsible when they are involved with decisions requiring **mediation** and **facilitation,** and

- empowering individuals and teams that have the skills, expertise, and commitment for accepting interdependent roles and responsibilities within their sphere of influence. The leader will serve as either a **delegator** or an **ambassador** to these individuals and teams.

Some leaders may also have excellent decision-making skills and tools in the first four or five decision-making strategies as depicted in Figure 2.1, but they may be *"viewed as having a need to control,"* which is antithetical to the role of developer. Therefore, by contrast *controllers* will be perceived as:

- resolving the problems efficiently when making **arbitration** and **negotiation** decisions but will create a sense of co-dependency and self doubt for team members,

- orchestrating the resolution of problems enthusiastically and effectively when serving as a **mediator** and thus creating a sense of co-dependency and self doubt for team members, (These leaders' active involvement in the decision-making process may prevent them from moving to the facilitation role. Therefore, leaders keep the individuals or teams at the co-dependence level).

- calculating when individuals or teams can be trusted to make the *"right decisions"* before **delegating** decisions to them, thus causing individuals and teams to have a feeling that they have to prove they are worthy. This manipulating process places competent inde-pendent professionals in a dilemma—fight the system by getting involved in a power struggle with the leader, work around the system, leave the system, or just learn to "play it safe. "

Leaders who are or might be viewed as controllers need to be very reflective and analytical concerning their real attitudes and paradigms about members of their teams. Being aware and sensitive to these attitudes and paradigms is an important first step. The good news is that attitudes and perceptions can be changed!

The most appropriate strategies are dependent upon the needs, experiences, skills, and commitment levels of individuals and teams. The "best fit" represents the most appropriate strategy between the needs of the individuals or teams and the decision-making strategy used:

- An **ambassador** strategy should be used with self-directed, interdependent teams. Such teams are still functioning within a hierarchical system and need to have access to information and other relevant resources in order to achieve win-win solutions for the system. Because the teams within an organization may not be readily accessible to each other or even knowledgeable about their independent roles and responsibilities, there is a need for the leader to serve as an ambassador, that is as an envoy, an emissary, a representative, and as a symbol of shared organizational values.

- A **delegation** strategy is appropriate for interdependent individuals and teams when they have the knowledge, skills, time, and commitment to handle the problem, issue, or concern. Leaders can delegate the decision-making responsibility to them and know they will operate within established guidelines and achieve a win/win solution. As the team strives for a win/win solution for the system, they will be functioning interdependently.

- A **facilitation** strategy should be used if the individuals or teams involved are not secure enough to make the decision without the involvement and support of their leader. The role of the leader is to provide encouragement and support and to assist both parties in reaching a win/win decision within the established guidelines. The encouragement plus the success in achieving a win/win solution within the team promotes and encourages independence.

- A **mediation** strategy is similar to the facilitation strategy. However, in the mediation role the leader is more actively involved in the deliberations. The leader is actively involved helping the two parties understand each other's perspectives, seeking potential win/win solutions, and helping them formulate a win/win strategy. The leader is encouraging individuals and teams to accept more responsibility in resolving issues, thus helping them become more independent.

- A **negotiation strategy (together)** is appropriate when one or both parties are unable to reach a satisfactory compromise because one or both parties lack skills, experience, technical knowledge, or commitment. They depend on the leader to bring the two parties together and to convince one or both parties to modify their position so that a satisfactory compromise can be achieved, although the solution may be perceived as win/lose by one or both parties.

- A **negotiation strategy (one-on-one)** is appropriate when one or both parties are not willing to "work through" the problem in a group setting or when bringing the two parties together is dysfunctional. The leader conducts a series of one-on-one meetings until a satisfactory resolution is achieved. Not only is this strategy time-consuming for the leader, the resolution will also likely be perceived as win/lose by one or both parties.

- An **arbitration** strategy is the last resort. The leader tries to resolve an issue when one or both parties are both unable to resolve the issue and they are unwilling to deal with the issue in a constructive manner. Because of a lack of knowledge and experience for this particular problem, they want the problem resolved but are unable to make a meaningful contribution. Therefore, the leader needs to make the decision, clarify expectations, and follow-up appropriately. Unfortunately for the leader, one or both parties may regard the solution imposed to be a "lose." Therefore, this can result in a lose/lose for all parties concerned.

The functional or the "best fit" between the needs of the individuals or teams and the decision-making strategy that should be employed is identified in Figure 2.1 on page 36. The continuum for the levels of "best fit" range from "1-1" to "7-7" where 1-1 and 7-7 represent:

- "1-1": Using the lowest level strategy "1," the leader will be the arbitrator and will tell one or both parties to modify their behavior. This strategy is the most appropriate when the members are at a lowest level "1" in terms of competencies and motivation. Therefore, the "1-1" is the leadership strategy that represents the best fit for the leader and concerned parties.

- "7-7": Using the highest level strategy "7," the leader will serve as an ambassador for those teams that are competent, committed, and able to function interdependently at level "7" with other teams. Therefore, the "7-7" is the leadership strategy that represents the best fit for the leader and concerned parties. An incompatible or dysfunctional fit would be a leadership strategy that did not match the needs of the participants. For example, as may be derived from Figure 2.1, a "1-6" would represent a leadership strategy of arbitration (1) with individuals that are able to function as interdependent teams (6). Therefore, a "1-6" arbitration strategy would be totally inappro-priate for this team.

Based upon this theoretical construct, the key to effective decision-making is to increase the skill and commitment levels of the participants throughout the organization. The increased commitment level is visually depicted in Figure 2.1 by the shaded area below the diagonal line. This shaded area represents the amount of time team members are willing to invest in the decision-making process and is a function of their skill and commitment levels. Therefore, this area also depicts the degree to which the leader is developing and using the leadership capacity within the organization.

At point "Z" members are both willing and able to solve the problem, and they are willing to invest whatever time it takes to resolve the issue. By contrast, at point "A" members are unable to solve the problem and are also psychologically unwilling to attempt the resolution because they do not have the knowledge, skills, or background. Therefore, they want the leader — or anyone — to "fix it"!

From the leader's perspective, the area above the diagonal line is equally important because it represents the amount of time required for monitoring the decision after it has been made. A team member at point "A" is not willing or able to make the decision; therefore, once the decision has been made by the leader, the leader will also be responsible for monitoring the decision. By contrast, the team member at point "Z" will spend whatever time is necessary for resolving the issue; therefore, the team accepts full responsibility and the leader does not need to monitor the decision.

At any point on the diagonal between points A and Z, one can see that the amount of time for monitoring a decision decreases as the amount of time team members are willing to commit to the resolution of the decision. This model highlights the importance of providing training for team leaders and team members throughout the organization, thus building leadership capacity throughout the system.

At the application level, effective leaders need to convey in writing and in their day-to-day practice a leadership belief statement that communicates the organization's commitment to effective decision-making. The following principle and belief statements are based on the conceptual framework presented in Figure 2.1:

PRINCIPLE:

People and organizations have the freedom to choose and are responsible for their choices, and choices rather than circum-stances control outcomes. Based on this principle:

LEADERSHIP BELIEF #2

We believe all decisions should be made at the most appropriate level in the organization and should be as close to the point of implementation as possible. The competency and commitment levels of those involved will help determine the appropriate level.

As leaders build the capacity of their organizations, the preference and frequency of use for these decision-making strategies should be in the following order: ambassador, delegator, facilitator, mediator, negotiator, and arbitrator.

- When individuals and teams have the competencies and commitment to function interdependently with other teams and the system as a whole, the leader should fulfill the role of ambassador.

- When individuals and teams have the competencies and commitment to function independently as a team, the leader should delegate the task to a team leader or team. If the task has implications for other teams, the leader should encourage them to think interdependently.

- When members are competent but insecure or uncommitted to make the decision without support, the leader should assist the individual or teams by serving as a facilitator or mediator.

- When members lack the competence but are committed to helping make the decision, the leader needs to serve as a negotiator and help forge a satisfactory compromise.

- When members do not have the requisite knowledge, skills, or motivation, the leader should serve as an arbitrator and make the decision.

  When leaders believe a decision may have "fallen outside the parameters" described in Leadership Belief #1, they have an obligation to:

  o approach the issue from a win/win perspective,

  o help the individual or individuals understand why they believe the decision is not within the existing parameters, and

  o if appropriate help the individual(s) or teams involved to modify or reverse the decision in such a way that their integrity is enhanced rather than diminished.

When leaders use these strategies effectively, they are ensuring that quality decisions are made throughout the organization. Furthermore, they are also increasing leadership capacity by empowering individuals to progress from dependence to independence to interdependence.

CHAPTER 3

DEVELOPING EMPOWERED INTERDEPENDENT INDIVIDUALS AND TEAMS

Effective leaders have a responsibility for influencing the quality of decisions throughout their organization. They find themselves in the dynamic position of trying to increase the capacity of individuals and teams by empowering them but at the same time recognizing their organizational responsibility to counterbalance individual and team empowerment with the requirement for hierarchical accountability. Therefore, the challenge for highly effective leaders is to balance that delicate tension between empowerment from below and organizational accountability and control from above.

Incorporating Belief Statements #1 and 2 into the fabric of the organization is helpful and provides a common framework for deliberating challenging organizational decisions. Leadership Belief #2 creates the expectation that decisions will be made as close to the point of implementation as possible while Leadership Belief #1 identifies the prerequisite conditions for those decisions, i.e, data based, sound theory and practice, etc. Those members who are closest to the point of implementation are the internal stakeholders who are going to be instrumental and responsible for applying the decision—making the decision work. In many cases, decisions within the context of these two leadership belief statements reinforce each other. However, in other cases, it places leaders and the organization in a potential win/lose position.

In order to fulfill the expectations of both Leadership Belief Statements 1 and 2, there must be a dynamic interaction between leaders and members of their teams that is supported and reinforced by the organization's systems and structures. The context for this interaction is in the power or influence arena that exists between leader and team members.

If *power* means "the capacity to influence outcomes," then by definition, leaders have power. Formal leaders have position power based on the legitimate authority of their position and are held accountable for quality decisions. In addition to position power, they have personal power based on individual characteristics that can positively influence others to support organizational goals.

It is also possible and desirable for leaders and team members to willingly commit themselves to the most *power-full* influence on behavior and attitude—principle-centered power. Principle-centered power is the desire to "make a difference," which serves as the inspiration, the motivation to commit to personal and organizational purposes that will have lasting influence.

As leaders empower individuals and teams appropriately, the level of problem-solving adequacy will increase proportionately; however, when individuals and teams are empowered beyond their levels of experience and/or expertise, problem-solving adequacy within their work units will be compromised. Likewise, when leaders overuse the authority of their office to make decisions rather than empowering individuals appropriately, the quality of decisions is also compromised. Inappropriate use of power inevitably has a negative impact on morale and problem-solving adequacy.

47

Therefore, the challenge for highly effective leaders is to manage the delicate balance between:

- boundary-stretching decisions resulting from empowerment of individuals and teams, and

- the leader's responsibility for organizational accountability.

This may be described as managing the balance between the leader's perceived need for continuity and the team's perceived need for change. In order to preserve continuity for accountability, the leader may feel the need to impose position power strategies for direction and guidance; whereas the team may feel the need for increased responsibility and a *power-with* approach to effect change. This tension may also result from the leader's perceived need for change and the team's desire for continuity. Regardless, there will be the need for the leader to manage and balance forces for continuity and change. Some examples of when this tension may exist include:

- a recommendation is forthcoming from the team that is not acceptable to the leader, (Should the leader stand firm? What "power tools" have the greatest potential to help achieve a win/win solution?)

- the team makes a decision that is unacceptable to the leader, (What should the leader do? Should the leader use the power of his/her office to overturn the decision? What "power tools" have the greatest potential to help achieve a win/win solution?)

- a recommendation is forthcoming from the leader that the team opposes, (What should team members do? What "power tools" can members and leaders use to capitalize on these differences?), and

- a leader has made a decision that is not supported by his/her team. (Members of the team complain to the next level and want the issue to be resolved in their favor. What should the leader do? What "power tools" can be used to "work through" this difference?)

When leaders are faced with problems, they must choose an appropriate power base to influence the behaviors of team members toward mission accomplishment. As illustrated in Figure 3.1 on page 51, the initial power strategy chosen will be determined by the leader's perception of the team members' need for:

- **growth by direction,** characterized by the leader translating the organizational mission and goals for team members. Because team members are demonstrating highly dependent behaviors and attitudes, the leader appropriately provides direction and guidance to gain compliance for mission-focused expectations. This typically necessitates the leader translating goals for team members by detailing what to do, how to do it, when to do it, and why to do it using *power-over* strategies, or

- **growth by collaboration,** characterized by the leader transacting with team members for utilitarian purposes. Both leader and individual team members know what a "win" is for them but recognize that in order to get what they want, they must substantially comply with the wishes of the other. Therefore, the leader must help them work toward a win/win solution using *power-with* strategies that will result in mission-driven behaviors that are reciprocally beneficial; or

- **growth by delegation,** characterized by both leader and members of interdependent teams demonstrating mutual respect, trust, and honor to the extent that they are willing not just to work for a win for themselves but are also willing to work to insure that the other parties get their win by utilizing *power-beyond* strategies.

At the highest level of interdependence, leaders and interdependent teams serve as ambassadors for each other and for the organization. They realize that by such advocacy for each other they are able to use their inherent independent diversity to interdependently achieve synergy.

By working for "not my way or your way, but a better way" they can truly achieve synergy, the creative innovations necessary to transform organizations and keep them viable and relevant to constantly changing stakeholder needs.

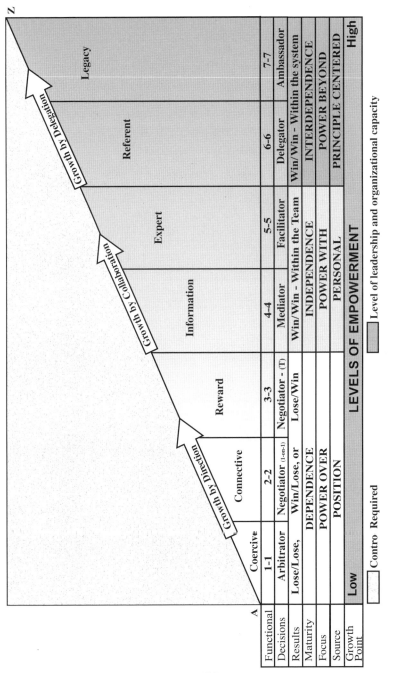

	Coercive	Connective	Reward	Information		Expert	Referent	Legacy	
Functional	1-1	2-2	3-3	4-4		5-5	6-6	7-7	
Decisions	Arbitrator	Negotiator (1-on-1)	Negotiator - (T)	Mediator		Facilitator	Delegator	Ambassador	
Results	Lose/Lose,	Win/Lose, or	Lose/Win	Win/Win – Within the Team		Win/Win – Within the Team	Win/Win – Within the system		
Maturity		DEPENDENCE		INDEPENDENCE			INTERDEPENDENCE		
Focus		POWER OVER		POWER WITH			POWER BEYOND		
Source		POSITION		PERSONAL			PRINCIPLE CENTERED		
Growth Point	Low			**LEVELS OF EMPOWERMENT**				High	

Growth by Direction

Growth by Collaboration

Growth by Delegation

☐ Contro Required

▨ Level of leadership and organizational capacity

Figure 3.1 : Growth Through Empowerment

51

As illustrated in Figure 3.1, the foundation for this model is the "power bases" that leaders have at their disposal:

- **position power,** that is, *power-over* others, by virtue of the inherent authority of their position;

- **personal power,** that is, *power-with* others, by virtue of the influence of their recognized knowledge and ability; and

- **principle-centered power,** that is, *power-beyond* others, by virtue of their intrinsic motivation of overarching purposes symbolized by principle-centered personal and organizational mission.

Leaders appropriately use *power-over* strategies authorized by their position when they perceive the need to translate organizational goals to unit members for the purpose of directing their efforts toward mission accomplishment. However, *power-over* strategies are sometimes driven by the temptation of efficiency whereby leaders can gain quick compliance by imposing the power of their position and instilling fear of reprisal for non-compliance.

Regardless of the rationale for using *power-over* strategies, their long-term impact will be negative reactive attitudes and behaviors associated with the perception of being controlled. Such strategies can be expected to yield minimal mission results, and the corporate culture can become one of "Employers pay just enough so that employees won't quit, and employees work just enough to avoid being fired."

Leaders demonstrate *power-with* strategies authenticated by **personal** competencies and qualities. They are using *power-with* strategies when they perceive the need to facilitate and coordinate the work efforts of others through making their information and expertise available. In order to maintain this power base, leaders must insure that their knowledge and skill base remains current and relevant and that they model the application of the competencies expected of others.

Principle-centered strategies are fueled by the goal of long-term proactive influence through having achieved worthy principle-centered purposes. Leaders motivated by the desire to leave a legacy use referent power. Leaders may not only demonstrate desirable professional competencies but also may exemplify positive personal character for the purpose of establishing influence.

They want to be trusted and respected, but their ultimate motive is to influence others to commit to common principles and purposes, that is, for team members to want to align their attitudes and behaviors with the mission, vision, and values. Therefore, this is not superficial support just to gain the favor of the leader; rather it is the intrinsic motivation to work with the leader toward mission accomplishment because they see the same needs and they share the same beliefs.

The model in Figure 3.1 builds upon the maturity levels of team members and the "best fit" or functional leadership strategy from Figure 2.1. In the model the maturity levels refer to the growth continuum of Dependence to Independence to Interdependence. When team members are functioning at the dependency level, they are demonstrating low levels of competency and commitment, which requires leaders to provide direction and guidance.

At the independent level, members have the necessary competence and commitment for mission accomplishment. However, they typically need the leader to support their efforts and to encourage them to recognize that they can accomplish more through working collaboratively in interdependent relationships than they can by competing independently.

In addition to the three broad growth-producing bases of power, this model identifies seven different "tools" that leaders can and should use depending upon the specific needs of those involved. In this model the "best fit" refers to diagnosing the level of competency and commitment for team members and then using the most appropriate "power tool." To be most effective, leaders need to use the most appropriate tool for the purpose of building leadership capacity. The seven tools and a brief definition of terms will be listed from the highest to the lowest forms of power:

- **Growth by Interdependent Delegation**

    o **Legacy Power** — leaders can use legacy power as a tool by building consensus among and serving as an ambassador for interdependent teams who are motivated by a commitment to leaving a legacy. In that environment, interdependent leaders and teams can truly transform organizations and leave a legacy worthy of emulation.

When commitment to principles and purposes has been promoted and exemplified by a trustworthy leader, the potential result is that the ambassador role becomes a mutual role between interdependent leaders and teams because they trust and need each other.

o **Referent Power** — Leaders can earn trust and confidence over time so that members know they can count on their leaders and trust them explicitly. Personally respected leaders can use members' desire to emulate and please them to create support for organizational mission and purposes by articulating, modeling, and symbolizing the principles that underpin the mission, vision, and values.

Leaders' appropriate use of referent power can facilitate the transition from growth by collaboration to growth by interdependent delegation. The leader's purpose is to encourage commitment not to self but rather to the principles and purposes of the organization.

- **Growth by Collaboration**

  o **Expert Power** – Independent teams and team leaders can be expected to rely on the expertise of their leader.

When leaders demonstrate first-hand knowledge and experience regarding a specific task, individuals will recognize the leader as one who has this valuable expertise.

As with information power, the leader is able to facilitate and coordinate the efforts of unit members to the extent that they value and use the leader's input.

o **Information Power** – Proactive leaders place themselves in positions of having access to accurate, valuable, and relevant information. This information places the leader in a position of leadership and influence.

Because independent teams and team leaders are typically intrinsically motivated, the leader can expect to be able to use his/her information to facilitate mission-focused transactions.

- **Growth by Direction**

  o **Reward** – Leaders are also in a position to acknowledge and to reward individuals and groups who are achieving the goals of the organization. The challenge for the leader is foster movement from growth by direction to growth by coordination.

  The appropriate use of reward power can promote the transition from extrinsic to intrinsic motivation for mission accomplishment.

o **Connective** – Because of their position, leaders are also able to connect less committed and/or less competent dependent individuals with influentials internal and external to the organization to encourage individual growth.

o **Coercive** – Leaders are in a position to use the power of their office to gain compliance. This is a last resort, but sometimes necessary, strategy leaders use to gain compliance for mission accomplishment from less competent and uncommitted individuals.

These tools need to be matched with the readiness or commitment levels of individuals and teams. When the leader misdiagnoses the appropriate level and therefore uses an inappropriate tool, undesirable results will occur.

For example, consider the impact of the following "mismatches":

- It would be dysfunctional for a leader to use coercive power to gain compliance from an individual who is competent and committed to make a quality decision.

- It would also be dysfunctional for a leader to use expert power with an individual who is neither competent nor committed to make an appropriate decision.

At the application level, effective leaders need to clarify and build these empowerment strategies into the day-to-day operations of their work units.

The following principle and belief statement are designed to help leaders balance and capitalize on the tension between accountability and responsibility:

PRINCIPLE:

>**Trust empowers others. Based on this principle:**

LEADERSHIP BELIEF #3

>**We believe our behavior should promote and encourage empowerment throughout our organization. Empowerment should be highly individualized and be a function of their development on the maturity continuum within the context of Leadership Belief #1.**

>**Over time, our preference and frequency and use of these power tools should be in the following order:**

>- Legacy,
>- Referent,
>- Expert,
>- Information,
>- Reward,
>- Connective, and
>- Coercive.

Consider a historical perspective for why and how leaders use power. The power model of the Industrial Age focused on exercising position power vested in hierarchical authority, typically resulting in a culture of compliance, control, and dependency created by *power-over* strategies. However, the advent of the Information Age has triggered a paradigm shift with leaders' use of power to a personal base with power vested in the individual's knowledge and expertise.

With influence vested in personal competencies, organizations are challenged to insure that positions are filled with individuals who can not only exercise legitimate power but who can also influence others through what they know and can do. This shift creates the potential for a culture of independency, which is a prerequisite for developing collaboration and interdependence, a culture consistent with the demands of a global economy.

This *power-with* approach has the added potential for developing leadership capacity within organizations when leaders facilitate the growth of team members from dependence to independence. This is also a culture where those individuals who are motivated by legacy power feel comfortable and are anxious to ally themselves with leaders and others who are similarly committed.

It is through those willing alliances where the energy for interdependent work emerges. Once leaders and team members are functioning at the interdependent level, they are more likely to be willing to serve as ambassadors for each other in order to foster and preserve the synergy in their relationships.

Leaders are always in the position of increasing and/or decreasing their power or influence potential. The power paradigm of some leaders is that power is finite, that is, "There is just so much power associated with my position and person; therefore, if I share power with others, then my amount of power is diminished."

Such a scarcity mindset will cause leaders to want to protect their vested power interests. By contrast, other leaders operate from the mindset, "The more power I share appropriately, the more power I have." They have an abundance mentality regarding power and are eager to share their power.

The leader's influence potential and the leadership capacity of the organization are increased when leaders use the most appropriate tool for helping individuals grow and develop.

CHAPTER 4

DEVELOPING COHESIVE TEAMS — BUILDING COMMUNITY

"United we stand, divided we fall! If we don't hang together, we will hang separately!"

The above statements highlight the significance of working together and sticking together. Effective leaders are responsible for ensuring that teams throughout their organization are functioning effectively. In our research we have found that the level of cohesiveness within organizations has a direct and powerful correlation with levels of productivity. Therefore, time and energy devoted to developing cohesive teams would be a pragmatic and proactive way to improve performance.

For example, as critics of public education continue to focus on perceived low performance, it would seem appropriate to consider how increasing levels of organizational cohesiveness could address some of their critical concerns. At the core of much of the current dissatisfaction is an implicit question, "How public are public schools?"

Does the public really own public schools? Some critics of public education would maintain that public schools are government owned and controlled. Others would say that they belong to the professional educational establishment. Few parents and patrons would suggest that public schools belong to them. In fact, in many communities, parents feel disenfranchised, ostracized, and alienated. In those cases, public schools are *in* the community but are not *of* the community. Reconciliation is unlikely unless school leaders change their paradigm of school-community relations and see the school as an authentic community organization and see their roles as community leaders.

Strategies for building authentic community between organizations and their public are beyond the scope of this discussion; however, it is our belief that developing cohesiveness within the organization is a prerequisite. Therefore, the focus of this chapter is on strategies for building cohesiveness—authentic communities—at the organizational level. Those endeavors will require more than just cosmetically using the label in the mission statement and putting members in teams.

Organizations will be into authentic community when shared vision and values are reflected both in policies and practices, when shared mission transforms a collection of independent "I's" to a collaborative of interdependent "we's" who are bonded together with a sense of identity and belonging. If the potential for becoming a "we" is stronger than the inclination to remain an "I," then when community based structures are offered, people will accept them.

In authentic communities the leadership mindset emphasizes *power-with* rather than *power-over* for the purpose of creating the *power-beyond* to accomplish shared missions and visions. The obligation and opportunity to lead are shared by all, a community of leaders. Leadership in communities is "inside-out." It is more *being* than *doing.*

Building a cohesive organization takes time, and it requires that both policy level and administrative level leadership place a premium on supporting and facilitating the development of cohesiveness within the organization. For example, at the campus level, the following teams are typically integral to efforts to improve cohesiveness throughout the school:

- administrative team,
- site-based teams, and
- departmental teams or grade level teams.

Unresolved issues within any of these teams create divisiveness within these teams as well as the teams these leaders represent and/or those they are connected to through the formal or informal networks. If there are unresolved issues at the top of the organization, the divisiveness of those issues can be expected to permeate the entire organization. Individuals are being asked in a variety of ways to "choose up sides."

Based upon our previous work, we have found that there are specific identifiable factors that impede the development of cohesive teams. Leaders are in a position to reflectively consider the degree to which these factors may be impacting the levels of cohesiveness of individual teams as well as the total system.

These factors or barriers are:

- unclear mission and goals,
- unrealistic goals,
- unclear messages about leadership and organizational values,

- mixed messages about leadership and organizational values,
- unstable structures,
- isolationism,
- negative competition,
- negative history,
- gamesmanship, and
- leader credibility.

Fortunately most of these factors are organizational in nature and leaders are in an excellent position to significantly impact them. Incorporating Leadership Belief Statements 1, 2, 3, and 4 into the fabric of the organization would be a proactive way to remove the negative impact of most of the factors identified above.

If a system is not in place for "working through" these unresolved issues, one can expect that the broader community will also become aware of or will be brought into these controversies. The internal and external image of organizations is greatly impacted by their levels of cohesiveness. Effective organizations have a way of keeping internal issues internal rather than allowing them to become public issues. A commitment to team building and working through issues at the appropriate level should be a priority.

Depending upon the stages of team development that are prevalent in the organization, leaders may not be aware of some of the internal conflicts. When they become aware, should they get involved in the internal disputes of teams they supervise directly and indirectly? When these "sticky" issues become known to leaders, they may respond with one or a combination of the following:

- Assume that interdependent teams and independent members of cohesive teams will "work through" these issues successfully,

- Listen to one or both parties and "coach" one or both parties on ways they could resolve the issue,

- Become involved with the team as a resource person and help them achieve a win/win solution,

- Provide support for the leader of the team and reinforce his/her efforts, or

- Convene the individuals or groups and clarify expectations and resolve the issue.

Figure 4.1 on page 66 graphically presents the theoretical framework for understanding the internal dynamics of building cohesive teams and the leadership role in the team building process. The model in Figure 4.1 builds upon the dependent, independent, and interdependent continuum from the three previous models and provides a framework for conceptualizing the stages of team development.

As presented in Figure 4.1, teams that have individuals who are functioning primarily in the dependent mode will by definition be functioning primarily in Stages 1 and 2. By contrast teams in Stages 5 and 6 have progressed to the highest level of cohesiveness and will function effectively as interdependent teams or as a professional community.

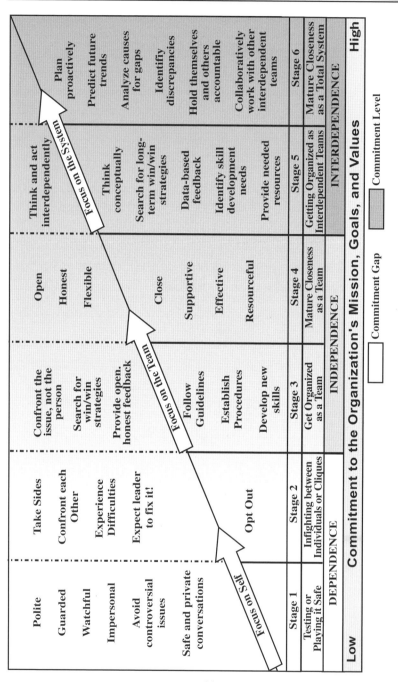

Figure 4.1: Stages of Team Development

The diagnosis of where individuals and teams are functioning on the dependent-independent-interdependent continuum provides a useful conceptual model for understanding the role of leaders and key members of the teams:

- When individuals and teams are *dependent* on their leaders, they are functioning either in the **testing** or the **infighting** stages. At the **testing** stage, leaders need to build in security and safeguards for them. At the *infighting* stage, they are dependent upon the leader to guide them through internal conflicts. The leaders need to help individuals view conflicts as natural and healthy and to help them move from win/lose thinking to win/win solutions. These win/win experiences help build a foundation that encourages individuals to move into the next stage.

- When individuals and teams are moving toward *independence* as a team, they are functioning in the **getting organized** and **mature closeness** stages. In the **getting organized** stage, leaders need to reinforce this independence by using a collaborative leadership style thereby helping the group focus its energies on confronting issues, establishing new procedures, and providing opportunities for team members to gain new knowledge and skills. These successful efforts reinforce the independence of individuals and the team as a whole. In the **mature closeness** stage of development, leaders need to reinforce their independence by serving as a resource person to the team upon request.

- When individual teams have experienced the fulfillment of mature closeness at the team level, they are now in a position where they can also experience *interdependence* and **mature closeness** within the broader work environment. This is much more complex and difficult to achieve than it is for an individual team because they are interacting with greater numbers of individuals and teams who have a greater diversity of potentially conflicting experiences and ideas.

  When these interdependent teams span organizational boundaries, they must also function without a common support structure. Therefore, there is the potential for an interdependent team to revert to infighting or getting organized as they strive to work with other independent or interdependent teams. Therefore, leaders need to assist these teams by encouraging them to be reflective and to again think and act interdependently.

  The leaders will need to serve as an ambassador for interdependent teams that are striving to work with other interdependent teams. These interdependent teams should function primarily in stages 5 and 6 as they fulfill an expanded leadership role with other independent and interdependent teams.

The shaded area below the diagonal line in Figure 4.1 represents team members' level of commitment to organizational goals. At point A, members are playing it very safe, and the goals of the organization are the least of their concerns because they are interested in personal survival. By contrast, at point "Z" individuals have achieved mature closeness within the total organization and are advocates for organizational mission, vision, and values.

The model in Figure 4.1 identifies the natural stages of team development. Teams throughout the organization will function primarily in one of the following stages of development:

> Stage 1: Testing or Playing it Safe as individuals,
>
> Stage 2: Infighting between individuals or cliques,
>
> Stage 3: Getting Organized as a team,
>
> Stage 4: Achieving Mature Closeness as a team,
>
> Stage 5: Getting Organized as interdependent teams, and
>
> Stage 6: Achieving Mature Closeness as a total system.

In Testing, members are concerned for personal safety and survival; therefore, their commitment to the goals of the unit is a secondary consideration at best. The task of leaders is to facilitate the movement of groups through these stages of development. With assistance, teams can move progressively through these six stages of development. However, without assistance, teams can "get stuck" in Testing or Infighting.

Every team or unit within an organization functions in one or a combination of these basic stages. The effectiveness of any group or unit in achieving its objectives is directly related to its developmental stage. Groups that function primarily in Stages 5 and 6 will be much more effective in achieving organization-wide objectives than those that get stuck in Stages 1 and 2.

Stage 1 is characterized by Testing or Playing It Safe. Every group or team goes through Stage 1 in the early stage of development. Individuals within the group will be:

- **polite,**
- **guarded,**
- **watchful,**
- **impersonal,**
- **avoiding discussion of substantive or controversial issues, and**
- **participating only in private, safe conversations.**

They feel they are unable to resolve the issue and therefore are unwilling to get involved. They will choose to play it safe and not get involved in controversial issues. For example, at the campus level, teachers will be thinking and or saying, "I am going back to my room, close my door, teach my class and not get involved in conflict." Until their "safety or security needs" have been met adequately within their team and/or the school, they will continue to play it safe in Stage 1.

Stage 2 is characterized by infighting. Members may be willing but not necessarily able to work through these differences without assistance. For example, initially some members may comply with the wishes of their team, but after gaining security, they will be willing to express some of their true feelings and may provide a very different perspective. When this occurs, they typically are suggesting that some existing practice or procedure should be changed. There are several possible consequences for these discussions:

- Individuals can easily get in a position where they **take sides** or are viewed as taking sides.

- Differences of opinion and/or disagreements can become personalized, and individuals can be viewed as **confronting each other.**

- Individuals who **experience difficulties** may want to **opt out** and to go back to a more secure and comfortable position in Stage 1.

- Frequently, "factions" within the team will go to the leader and expect the problem to get fixed— that is, to fix the problem their way!

The leader's response is crucial because infighting can be destructive, or it can be a growth opportunity for the team. If leaders and teams do not have procedures for working through internal issues, the infighting stage can become destructive causing individuals to physically or psychologically remove themselves from the infighting unit.

The leader's view or attitude toward conflict will dictate the direction of the team   regression or growth:

- If leaders dislike conflict, they will have a tendency to avoid the conflict and try to peacefully co-exist by using the one-on-one negotiation strategy. This leader response models and reinforces Stage 1 behavior.

71

- If leaders view conflict as natural and healthy, they will try to capitalize on these differences as a way to move their teams to Stage 3 by focusing on win/win solutions.

Stage 3 is characterized by getting organized as a team. Teams in Stage 3 are characterized by individuals who cannot work through these issues without the assistance of a leader who is external to the team. The external leader may serve as a resource person to the leader or team members prior to group meetings.

The leader could assist individuals in brainstorming potential strategies and "coach" them in ways to get to a win/win solution, thus encouraging the team to become more independent. The external leader could also participate in the meeting as a resource person and would fulfill the role of a facilitator or mediator.

In this role leaders will help individuals:

- **confront the issues** and not each other,
- search for **win/win strategies,**
- provide open, honest **feedback,**
- clarify the importance of everyone **following** existing **guidelines,**
- translate concerns into improved guidelines and **establish procedures,** and
- provide resources for new **skill development.**

Stage 4 is characterized by mature closeness as independent teams. The model provides a conceptual framework for identifying those behaviors that are characteristic of the mature closeness of independent teams. Individuals trust each other sufficiently to share their concerns openly. If an outside person observed this group at work, it would be difficult to determine the official leader because leadership is truly shared. Individual teams at this stage of development are highly productive because team members are:

- **open** and **honest** with each other,
- **flexible** and **resourceful** consistent with their values,
- **effective** in working as **team members,** and
- a **close and supportive** group.

Stage 5 is characterized by getting organized as interdependent teams. Interdependent teams in Stage 5 are characterized by teams and team leaders who want to positively influence other internal and external independent and interdependent teams. However, the complexity and size of the system may inhibit the opportunity and support for needed changes, which may cause frustration and temporarily cause them to regress to Stage 1 or 2.

The leader needs to provide support and assistance to team members by serving as a resource person to assist in brainstorming potential strategies and "coach" them in ways to return to win/win solutions, thus encouraging the team to again achieve interdependence. Because these teams have experienced the synergy associated with mature closeness and have the desire for wholeness and interdependence, they are in an excellent position to help the organization move to mature closeness as a system.

Therefore, they are ready to assume a delegated leadership role within the system to expedite the development and movement of other independent teams through Stages 3 and 4 and into Stage 5 by encouraging other teams to:

- **think** and act **interdependently,**
- **think conceptually,**
- search for **long-term** win/win **strategies,**
- provide **data-based feedback,** and
- identify needs of the team so that new **skills** can be **developed** and additional **resources provided.**

Stage 6 is characterized by mature closeness as **interdependent teams.** The model provides a conceptual framework for identifying those behaviors that are characteristic of mature closeness for interdependent teams for the system. Because of the complexity, sophistication, and inherent risk of some of these behaviors, these teams and team leaders need the assistance of the formal leader in an ambassador role.

The ambassador may need to skillfully exercise both personal and position power, demonstrate effective collaborative skills, and serve as a resource person. The ambassador role of the formal leader involves developing the leadership capacity within interdependent teams in order for them to also fulfill this vital ambassador role.

Interdependent teams encourage themselves and other interdependent teams to:

- work with other interdependent teams internal and external to the system,
- hold themselves and others accountable for the highest standards of mission accomplishment,
- identify discrepancies between stakeholder needs and mission purposes,
- analyze causes for gaps between actual and desired results,
- predict future trends, and
- plan proactively.

At the operational level, effective leaders need to clearly communicate their expectations for effective teamwork throughout their units. The following principle and leadership belief statement are based on sound theory and practice and can help leaders communicate this important concept to members throughout the organization:

PRINCIPLE:

The whole is greater than the sum of the parts. Based on this principle:

LEADERSHIP BELIEF #4

We believe we have an obligation to establish and maintain cohesive interdependent teams with a high commitment to the organization's mission and goals. Teams will assume leadership responsibility for identifying,

achieving, and monitoring the highest standards of performance consistent with student and other stakeholder needs by capitalizing on the strength and diversity of members and other interdependent teams.

Therefore, in order to improve cohesiveness leaders should:

a. In Stage 1 (Testing), design strategies that provide a safe, secure environment for team members.

b. In Stage 2 (Infighting), help members view differences of opinion and disagreements as natural and healthy and to help them work through these differences. Approaching these differences from a win/win perspective rather than win/lose is imperative. These differences of opinions create opportunities for releasing the synergy within groups. This synergy should promote cooperation rather than competitive-ness and should propel the group into Stage 3.

c. In Stage 3 (Getting Organized as a Team), use a collaborative leadership style and help the group focus its energies on confronting issues rather than individuals, on establishing procedures for improving existing conditions, and for providing opportunities for team members to gain new knowledge and skills.

d. In Stage 4 (Mature Closeness as a Team), incorporate themselves into the team as team members and truly share leadership. At this level of development, members of the team will feel comfortable initiating leadership acts, refocusing the group on issues, proposing improved ways of doing business, and assisting other team members in achieving quality.

e. In Stage 5 (Getting Organized as Interdependent Teams), delegate the autonomy to interdependent teams and encourage them to think and act interdependently, think conceptually, search for long-term win/win strategies, provide data-based feedback, and identify needs of the team so that new skills can be developed and additional resources provided.

f. In Stage 6 (Mature Closeness as Interdependent Teams), serve as ambassadors and work with other interdependent teams internal and external to the system. Members will hold themselves and others accountable for the highest standards of mission accomplishment, identify discrepancies between stakeholder needs and mission purposes, analyze causes for gaps between actual and desired results, predict future trends, and plan proactively.

CHAPTER 5

GRANTING AUTONOMY WITH INTERDEPENDENCE

Today public and private institutions are under the microscope and are being held more accountable for results than ever before. With this increased push for accountability from external sources, leaders are in a pivotal position. How they respond to the external pressure sends a powerful message throughout their organizations. If they are able to capitalize on these external pressures, they can use these pressures to help members see the need to adapt and change. The challenge for leaders is to be proactive, anticipate the need for change, and innovatively respond prior to the external demand; thus, individuals, teams, and the system as a whole can establish and/or maintain their professional autonomy.

How do leaders create an environment that encourages and promotes professional **freedom and responsibility** throughout their organization? What can leaders do to promote individual freedom in such a way that those freedoms will have a positive impact upon productivity for individuals and teams throughout the organization rather than creating individual freedom at the expense of organizational productivity?

The needs and rights of individuals vs. the needs of the group have been debated for decades. What should leaders do when they observe individual behaviors that are inconsistent or in conflict with the system-wide goals, rules and regulations, and/or the established parameters in Belief Statement #1?

As they try to help individuals and teams gain responsibility, leaders face a dilemma of whether or not to intervene because of anticipated and unanticipated consequences:

- If the leader does not intervene, the team member may be unaware that a "problem exists," and the dysfunctional behavior will probably continue. Other team members know the leader did not intervene; therefore, they may conclude that the behavior is acceptable and may choose to replicate the behavior. Those who thought the leader should have intervened, may conclude that "anything goes."

- If the leader does intervene but is perceived as doing so too quickly, the team members may be offended and decide to meet the letter of the law, not the intent of the law. When they "replay the experience" in the lounge, the parking lot, or on the web, "their spin" will probably characterize the leader as a "nit picker" or "control freak."

- The intervention may have been very timely and have helped the individual or team progress on the dependent-independent-interdependent continuum resulting in excellent short and long term results.

By choosing to intervene or not to intervene, leaders are making conscious choices about a commodity called autonomy, which is visually depicted in Figure 5.1. The leader's role in developing autonomy for individuals and teams throughout the organization is to bridge the gap from personal accountability to organizational responsibility.

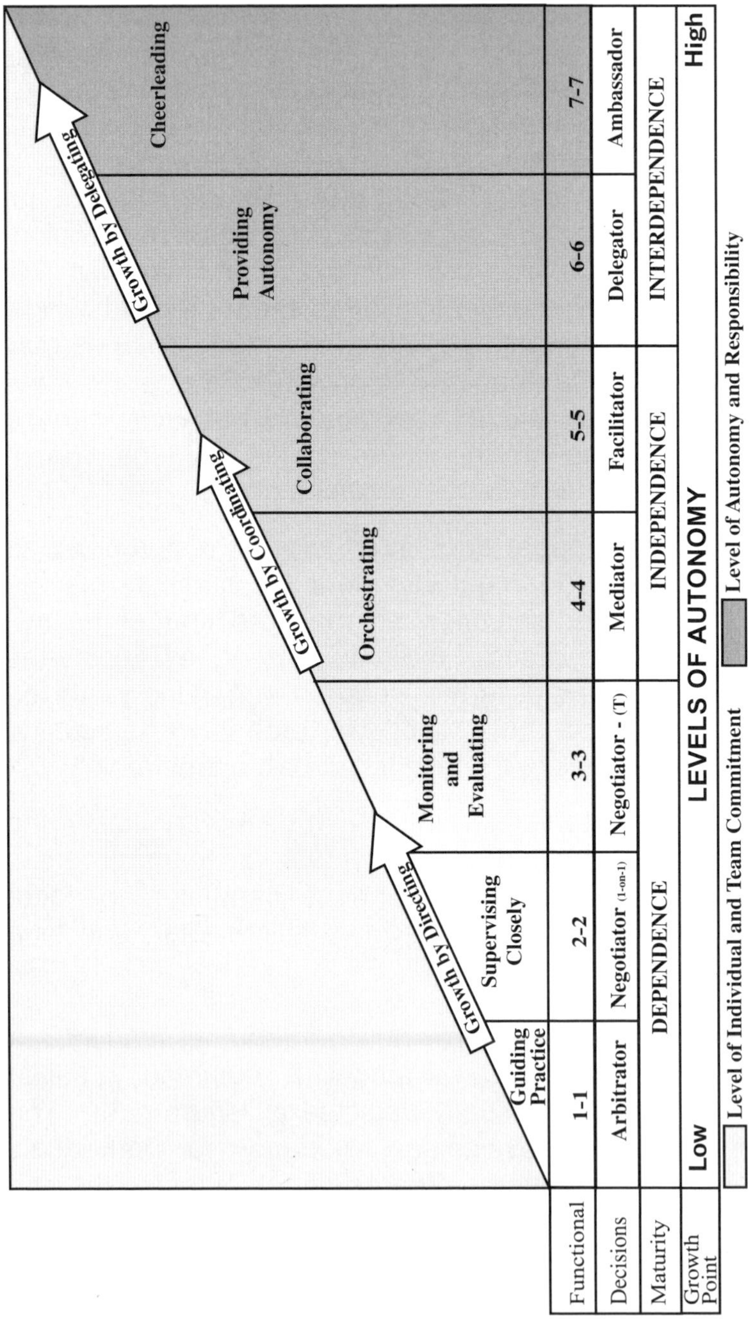
Growth by Directing
Growth by Coordinating
Growth by Delegating
Guiding Practice
Supervising Closely
Monitoring and Evaluating
Orchestrating
Collaborating
Providing Autonomy
Cheerleading
Functional
1-1
2-2
3-3
4-4
5-5
6-6
7-7
Decisions
Arbitrator
Negotiator (1-on-1)
Negotiator - (T)
Mediator
Facilitator
Delegator
Ambassador
Maturity
DEPENDENCE
INDEPENDENCE
INTERDEPENDENCE
Growth Point
Low
LEVELS OF AUTONOMY
High
Level of Individual and Team Commitment
Level of Autonomy and Responsibility

Figure 5.1: Moving From Accountability to Responsibility

As has been stated in previous chapters, leaders need to make a commitment to building the culture that encourages and promotes individuals and teams to grow through the stages of personal growth and development. To accomplish this objective, leaders need to know members of their teams so well that they can assist them in moving through these stages of development as shown in Figure 5.1.

From a leader perspective, it is imperative to know where individuals and teams are on the dependent—independent—interdependent continuum because it is prerequisite to determining the appropriate strategy to use to help these individuals function effectively and to move to higher levels:

- When individuals and teams are **dependent** upon the leader because of their lack of experience, knowledge, skills, or confidence, the leader has an obligation to help them grow by providing direction, structure, support, guidance, and appropriate supervision. Even within the dependence mode, the role of the leader will evolve from providing **guided practice** to **close supervision** to **monitoring** and **evaluating** thereby granting increased degrees of freedom and preparing individuals for future independence.

- When individuals move into levels 4 and 5 as depicted in Figure 5.1, they are ready to experience **independence** and accept the associated level of responsibility. This is a significant shift because individuals are moving from dependent accountability to independent responsibility. The leader's role is to provide individuals and teams. Coordination is important growth by coordinating the efforts of other because even with their newly established independence and perspective, they will not necessarily see either the interrelationships between themselves and their team members or between their team and other teams. Therefore, the leader will help fulfill this important role as a mediator or facilitator by assisting the team to establish standards of quality, procedures for feedback and evaluation, and strategies for interacting with other teams.

- Organizational productivity should increase significantly when individuals and teams move to levels 6-6 and 7-7 as depicted in Figure 5.1. These interdependent individuals will by definition have the requisite commitment and competencies for the specific tasks under consideration. Furthermore, additional professional growth will evolve from such interdependent individuals and teams. They will be committed to fostering interdependence within and between teams that can be expected to result in quality control and quality assurance strategies throughout their sphere of influence.

The most appropriate leadership strategies to facilitate movement of individuals and teams along the maturity continuum are dependent upon the needs, experiences, skills, and commitment levels of individuals and teams. As Figure 5.1 illustrates, the most effective leadership strategies are those that match the skill and commitment levels of participants. Those strategies along the growth continuum are labeled as Growth by Directing, Growth by Coordinating, and Growth by Delegating.

Growth by Directing: Dependence with Accountability

Within the strategies of growth by directing, leaders need to provide the necessary structure and support in order for individuals to progress through these three levels. Individuals who are new to an organization can be expected to begin in the Dependent Stage. They are dependent upon others to translate the formal and informal norms that guide the day-to-day operations within the organization. They are dependent upon the formal and informal leaders to provide structure, support, reassurance, etc. They typically want to know the "do's" and "don'ts."

An organization may also have long-term employees that are still functioning in the dependency mode. From their perspective, the dependency mode could be considered a safe mode because they are being directed by others, which fulfills their need for direction and support/security. Based on our experience we have found that the following strategies are effective in achieving accountability with dependent individuals:

- **Guiding practice** — If individuals are attempting to perform a new task and are unable to perform it by themselves, a leader needs to provide an opportunity for guided practice. Depending upon the nature of the task, guided practice could be provided by a designated mentor, team or department leader, or appropriate member of the administrative team.

- **Supervising closely** — After adequate guided practice, the individual is in a position to perform the task. However, depending upon the nature of the task and the frequency of replication, the individual still needs close supervision. The close supervision will provide accountability because it provides the opportunity to observe and correct a mistake early before it becomes incorporated into a person's mode of operation.

- **Monitoring and Evaluating** — Providing the structure and support for individuals in this stage is very important because one of the objectives is to help these individuals move toward independence. Early activities would include planning time with the leader who is providing the structure. Later the leader will ask more questions and will be helping individuals reduce their need for dependency. The structured evaluation sessions will provide an opportunity for candid feedback and will help the individual use the feedback to improve performance.

Growth by Coordinating: Developing Independence with Responsibility

Within the strategies of growth by coordinating, leaders need to build on individuals' motivation to function independently and to help them accept more responsibility. Therefore, the leader's role is to help them incorporate their independent decisions into the broader contexts of other teams and the system as a whole.

Based on our experience we have found that the following strategies are effective in achieving responsibility with independent individuals:

- **Orchestrating:** The role of the leader is help these individuals or teams in developing independence with responsibility. These individuals and teams will be able to function independently but will need someone to help them structure the interrelationships between their team and other teams within the organization. The leader is responsible for insuring that these interrelationships will not negatively impact other teams.

- **Collaborating:** The role of the leader is to help these individuals or teams to assume independence with responsibility and to start thinking interdependently. These teams will need someone to help them see the interrelationships both within their team and between other teams within the organization. Therefore, asking appropriate questions such as, "How do you think . . . will impact other teams within our system?" would be an example of a facilitative leadership style that should help teams develop win/win thinking.

Growth by delegating: Developing Interdependence within the Professional Community

Within the strategies of growth by delegating, leaders need to capitalize on individual and team commitment to mission, vision, and values by serving as their ambassador. Because these teams will be interacting with both internal and external teams that may not be functioning at the interdependent level, it is the leader's responsibility to serve as a resource and "cheerleader" for these synergistic efforts by:

- **Providing autonomy:** The role of the leader is to delegate appropriate responsibility to these interdependent individuals or teams. These individuals have demonstrated their ability to value the benefits of collaborating interdependently instead of competing independently and are now willing to accept responsibility as a team player.

- **Cheerleading:** The role of the leader is to serve as an ambassador for those individuals and teams who accept accountability for the standards, vision, and values of the organization. These individuals and teams serve as advocates for mission accomplishment both inside and outside the organization. They understand that a truly professional community is self-policing and that collaboration within the professional community will produce synergistic results. The leader reinforces their efforts to seek "third alternatives" from diverse sources inside and outside of the organization.

As described above and as previously depicted in **Figure 2.1: Decision-Making Model,** achieving the "best fit" between leadership strategies and the needs of individuals and teams will result in optimal growth from dependence to independence to interdependence. As is implied in this leadership growth continuum, the challenge for the leader is to use feedback to diagnose individuals and teams accurately so that both leader and team members are working at the highest possible maturity level. This is crucial because misdiagnosis inevitably results in either regression or dysfunction.

Appropriately diagnosing and leading along the growth continuum takes time, but as the model suggests, it is far more effective because it develops the capacity that enables the leader to move from the time intensive responsibility for dependent individuals to the gratifying role of observing and serving as an ambassador for synergistic interdependent teams.

At the application level, effective leaders need to convey both in policy and in practice a leadership principle and a belief statement that communicate the organization's commitment to increase the levels of autonomy. Such statements should clearly communicate the leader's commitment to move individuals and teams from accountability to responsibility.

PRINCIPLE:

> **Effective relationships require mutual benefit. Based on this principle:**

BELIEF STATEMENT #5

> **We believe our behavior should promote and encourage professional autonomy and growth from independence to interdependence for individuals and teams throughout the organization.**

In order to encourage professional autonomy within and between teams, we believe that:

- autonomy should be highly individualized,

- autonomy should be a function of the maturity levels of individuals and teams, and

- individuals who have gained autonomy have an obligation to balance the concepts of independence and interdependence.

When an independent decision has an impact upon another team within the organization or the unit as a whole, individuals should think "interdependence" rather than independence.

CHAPTER 6

ALIGNING STRUCTURES, SYSTEMS, AND STRATEGIES WITH MISSION

Leaders have an obligation to provide quality assurance and quality control for organizational members and all shareholders. Leaders are the designated "keepers of the vision" because they are in the best position to see the scope of the organization and its relevant relationship to the broader environment. In order to do so leaders must have feedback systems in place to help them maintain the vision; otherwise it is possible that they could be blinded by seeing "what they or others want to see" and therefore lose sight of reality. The focus for this chapter is to help the leader insure that the organization is properly aligned so that it can accomplish the mission efficiently and effectively.

Organizational alignment is in place when each of the individual components of the organization operates in harmony. Even though there are many components that comprise an organization that interact and impact each other, effective leaders view—and help others view—the organization holistically as an ecosystem rather than as a collection of individual pieces. It is common commitment to and alignment with the mission that causes independent organizational departments and components to operate interdependently. It is that interdependence that creates the culture for the synergy and innovation necessary for high productivity. Therefore, structures and systems must not just support but clear and pave the way for the mission and vision of the organization to be operationalized.

Leadership styles and skills must also be aligned with the values of the organization as extensions of the mission and vision. All of these components must be and remain connected with the needs of the stakeholders.

Primary alignment in an organization begins with each individual in the organization working to achieve an organizational mission that is consistent with the needs of the stakeholders. Primary alignment is analogous to individuals who are using personal computers as standalone workstations to meet customer needs. As with the human body, when a rib is cracked, it is painful, but does not short-circuit the system, just as when one computer goes down, it does not shut down the system.

Secondary alignment would transform those individual workstations into an interconnected network that provides intelligent structures and systems that facilitate individuals working in concert with other individuals in the organization. Although primary alignment directs and drives individuals in organizations toward mission accomplishment, secondary alignment provides structures and support systems that create an organizational environment that fosters and facilitates synergistic, interdependent efforts to meet stakeholder needs and to do so more efficiently and effectively.

In the human body, when the skeletal structure is out of alignment, pinched nerves and pain may occur and even paralysis can set in. In organizations, when structures and systems are not aligned with mission and stakeholder needs, efforts of individuals within the organization to meet those demands can be expected to cause "pain" both to the organization and to the individuals.

Consider the all-to-common scenarios of organizations that do not work at maintaining mission and values statements that are consistent with either the current environmental realities or with the needs and desires of its stakeholders:

- If the leaders of that organization maintain allegiance to a status quo mission that is irrelevant or at best inadequate from the perspective of the stakeholders, then it can be expected that the relationship between the organization and those in the outer environment will be less than harmonious because the organizational outputs do not meet stakeholder needs.

- Or consider the plight of an organization that does not seek to rally around any guiding values or mission and is routinely adopting the latest "hot" program-of-the-month.

With the primary alignment components in place, autonomous, independent individuals with the necessary character and competence for goal accomplishment can achieve results that satisfy stakeholders even if the organizational structures, systems, and strategies are not supportive. Autonomous, independent individuals in such organizations who want to produce relevant results for the stakeholders are forced to work around or over or through dysfunctional structures, systems, or staff. Interestingly, many authors have extolled those who "think outside the box" without realizing that "the box" is likely structures and systems in the organization that are out of alignment with the needs of the stakeholders. Therefore, proactive leaders need to provide structures that are freeing rather than confining so that "outside the box" thinking can be operationalized and "institutionalized."

Primary alignment is therefore a construct of vision and strategy. Independent efforts to attain primary alignment can become interdependent efforts when trustworthy individuals see the potential personal and organizational mutual benefits from working collaboratively rather than competing independently. As leaders facilitate movement on the growth continuum from independence to interdependence, they build upon shared commitment to mission, vision, and values. They see that trust based relationships can yield synergistic results when the collective "we" is committed to shared mission, vision, and values. Such interdependent teams can then be expected to adopt values and beliefs that are consistent with stakeholder needs. This movement on the growth continuum paves the way for secondary alignment of organizational structures and systems.

Secondary alignment of structures (organizational chart assigning authority and responsibility, staff roles and relationships, resources) and systems (communication, compensation, training, work processes) is essential for optimal performance. Therefore, once mission, vision, and values are defined, the leader's responsibility is to align the structure and systems to pave the path for mission and strategy to succeed.

The environment surrounding organizations is increasingly dynamic, and it contains the key needs and demands of stakeholders. That being the case, it is a necessary function of organizational leaders to maintain constant commerce with the environment, to understand it, and to predict future trends in it. The obvious impact of a dynamic environment on organizational secondary alignment is that structures and systems must also be dynamic if they are to remain in alignment.

Existing organizational structures and systems inevitably lead to the results that the organization is producing; therefore, the organization can be said to be perfectly aligned to get the results that it is getting. When a vehicle steers straight, it is aligned to do so; likewise, if that vehicle pulls to either the left or right, it is because it is aligned to do so. Even though the car is said to then be "out of alignment," it is perfectly aligned to pull to the left or right.

In organizations as with cars, misaligned systems lead to misaligned outcomes. Consequently, organizational leaders can only "steer" the organization straight on the path toward mission accomplishment if they have clear vision and know how to pave the path.

According to Stephen Covey there are "Six Rights" that define alignment:

- Right processes,
- Right structures,
- Right people,
- Right information,
- Right decisions, and
- Right rewards.[3]

Our adaptation of those Six Rights includes adding a Right, modifying a Right, changing the sequence, and applying these rights to educational settings. It is our assertion that an aligned system is one where the **right mission** is fulfilled by the **right people** working through the **right structures** with the **right processes** using the **right information** to make the **right decisions** followed by the **right consequences.** We believe that adding the **right mission** is absolutely critical to maintaining the focus and alignment consistent with "true north." Right Rewards has been expanded to **Right Consequences** in order to include not only personal rewards but also organizational accountability. Adding the **Right Mission** is consistent with our conceptual model in Figure 8.

We believe that the sequence of our "Seven Rights" is logically consistent with the concepts of primary and secondary alignment. Also, the reordering of Covey's Six Rights is supported by Peter Drucker's assertion that "Mission defines Strategy, after all, and Strategy defines Structure."[4] Further, these concepts have been specifically adapted to alignment issues within education.

As you examine these alignment issues, you will have an opportunity to be reflective concerning the degree to which these practical, day-to-day issues are aligned within your work unit. Later you may want to make copies of the item statements in Appendix A in order to critically examine these issues.

The response choices in Appendix A are: **Out of Alignment, Partial Alignment, Excellent Alignment, and Unsure.** The exercise will be an opportunity for you and members of your team to record the degree to which there is alignment on these issues.

Right Mission

The right mission is one that is aligned with the primary needs and concerns of organizational stakeholders.

Because the environment surrounding organizations is increasingly dynamic, leaders must maintain constant commerce with it, understand it, and be able to anticipate shifting trends in it. The obvious impact of a dynamic environment on organizational secondary alignment is that structures and systems must also be dynamic if they are to remain in alignment. Please consider:

- To what extent is our organization's mission aligned with the needs of current and future stakeholders?

- To what extent are our mission, vision, and values aligned with the expectation of *"Learning for all, whatever it takes"*?

- To what extent is our organization's mission aligned with my personal mission?

- To what extent are my job responsibilities aligned with our organization's mission?

Right People

Primary alignment emanates from the personal level. The right people are those who demonstrate both character and competence (trustworthiness) because they will engender trust in others and are able to act and lead effectively. The right people are those who seek opportunities to develop both character and multiple competencies. Leaders who understand how to build a high-trust environment will positively influence the effectiveness of the organization. Please consider:

- To what extent are our personnel policies, procedures, and actual practices aligned to insure that the right people are employed?

- To what extent are our personnel policies, procedures, and actual practices aligned to insure that the right people are retained and developed?

- To what extent are our personnel policies, procedures, and actual practices aligned to promote job enlargement opportunities?

Right Structures

Aligned structures (organizational chart assigning authority and responsibility, staff roles and relationships, and resources) provide the organizational flexibility to be able to assemble the right individual or group based on the needs of the situation. This is a matter of both responsibility and relationships. Some situations, especially crises, dictate top down hierarchical initiative and responsibility; whereas the desired results in other situations can best be developed through a team structure. Please consider:

- To what extent are our roles and responsibilities aligned with our goals?

- To what extent are rules and regulations aligned with our goals?

- To what extent is our curriculum vertically aligned?

- To what extent do the structures encourage alignment across content areas? (In other words, is our content contained in isolated silos or integrated across disciplines?)

- To what extent are resources such as technology aligned with our priorities? (In other words, are our resources assigned on a need basis or on a personal basis?)

- To what extent is our agenda for organizational meetings aligned with our goals?

- To what extent do our structures support tasks? (Is there an appropriate mix between command-and-control structure and team structure?)

- To what extent is "what we say" aligned with "what we do"?

Right Processes

Right processes should facilitate people working effectively together, focus their efforts on efficient mission related behaviors, and provide autonomy to adjust strategies at the point of customer interface. Please consider:

- To what extent are our vertical leadership teams' decisions aligned with our commitment to shared interdependent decision-making?

- To what extent are our horizontal team's decisions aligned with our commitment to shared interdependent decision-making?

- To what extent do our leadership teams above align feedback with technological capacity? (In other words, are they using technology-based strategies such as email, list-servs, intra-web networks, chat-rooms, etc. for feedback purposes?)

- To what extent are our decisions/deliberations made in staff meetings aligned with our stakeholders' priorities?

- To what extent are information technologies inside our organization aligned with information technologies outside our organization?

Right Information

For many the Information Age means information overload; therefore, a requisite skill of Information Age workers is the ability to discern what is necessary to know from that which is nice to know. The leader's responsibility is to have communications systems in place that make accurate information—both data and feedback—accessible to those in the organization who need it first. Please consider:

- To what extent is access to relevant information aligned with the needs of decision-makers?

- To what extent is there alignment between the authority to make decisions and access to relevant and accurate data?

- To what extent is there alignment between the practice of open, honest information sharing and the need for confidentiality of private/sensitive information?

- To what extent is there alignment between the important practice of reporting minutes from official meetings and the need for open, honest but private dialogue? (For example, are minutes of official meetings restricted only to a record of actions taken or do they include a reporting of "who said what about whom"?)

- To what extent is there alignment between what is said *to* people and what is said *about* people?

Right Decisions

As Leadership Belief Statement #2 says, *"We believe all decisions should be made at the most appropriate level in the organization and should be as close to the point of implementation as possible."*   Those in the organization who need access to accurate information first are those who have frontline interface with stakeholders and shareholders in the outer environment; therefore, implementing Belief Statement #2 will help insure that the best choices are made by those with the most knowledge and expertise. Please consider:

- To what extent is there alignment between Leadership Belief #2 (decisions made at the appropriate level) and actual practice?

- To what extent is there alignment between the concept of "those impacted by the decision should be involved in the decision" and actual practice?

- To what extent is there alignment between the trust vested in people and their demonstrated trustworthiness?

- To what extent is there alignment between leaders' styles and skills and the practice of decisions being made at the appropriate level?

- To what extent is authority for decision-making commensurate with responsibility?

Right Consequences

It is the leader's responsibility not only to insure that the right people get the right information necessary for right decisions but also that the consequences of those decisions are aligned with actual performance. In other words, consequences should be clearly aligned with results. Please consider:

- To what extent is there alignment between the compensation system and the demonstrated performance of people?

- To what extent are benefits aligned with actual needs of people? (For example, is the benefit plan flexible enough to accommodate individual needs?)

- To what extent is there alignment between the criteria for advancement and demonstrated job performance? (For example, is movement to a higher role viewed as the result of competency or a reassignment based upon marginal success?)

- To what extent is there alignment between the quality of performance and performance evaluation data?

- To what extent is there alignment between the evaluation data and recognition for effectiveness?

- To what extent is there alignment between the evaluation data and consequences for poor performance?

- To what extent is there alignment between the evaluation data and the staff development component?

- To what extent is there alignment between student progress reporting and our mission, vision, and values?

Although we have identified "Seven Rights" as the critical alignment issues, these components operate not in isolation from but in concert with each other—as an ecosystem. Although primary alignment can be achieved through the efforts of independent individuals, secondary alignment of structures, systems, and "Rights" is dependent on effective leadership. Therefore, leadership styles and skills must also be aligned with the "Rights" of the organization in order to insure that quality assurance and quality controls exist throughout the organization.

Commitment to the following belief statement from every level becomes the stabilizing and integrating force in the organization. The following principle and belief statement are based on sound theory and practice and can help leaders communicate this important concept to members throughout the organization:

PRINCIPLE:

Quality Production (results) requires continual development of production capability. Based on this principle:

BELIEF STATEMENT #6

We believe that we have an obligation to build in quality control and quality assurance strategies throughout the organization. Building feedback loops into the system will assist leaders in aligning mission, strategies, structures, and systems to ensure quality control and assurance throughout the organization.

Since the leader's ability to know and understand alignment issues is requisite to insuring that organizational results are consistent with the mission, utilizing the "Right" questions will allow leaders to analyze the perceptions of others regarding primary and secondary alignment issues. As you reflect upon your perceptions to the "Seven Rights" you are encouraged to:

- respond to the item statements in Appendix A and determine the degree to which these seven rights are present in your organization,

- identify those areas that you believe could be brought into alignment fairly easily through your leadership (secondary alignment),

- identify those areas in which it would be helpful to have feedback from members of your teams,

- develop an overall strategy for improving alignment, and

- prioritize the alignment issues. (If the "mission" issue is out of alignment, you are encouraged to start with the basics.)

These data can become the catalyst to assist you and members of your organization in redesigning and/or reengineering relationships between people, processes, and purpose.

CHAPTER 7

FUNCTIONING IN THE "FISH BOWL"

As leaders and team members fulfill their roles in their organizations, they are functioning within a fishbowl. What patrons "see" officials doing—or not doing—impacts the image and reputation of the organization. Many of the things leaders do, or do not do, are highly visible to individuals throughout the organization and even to the broader community. For example, since principals are being held accountable for operating a safe and productive campus, their behavior within the fishbowl is scrutinized carefully. This scrutiny comes from within the school, outside of the school, and from central office personnel from above. Like it or not, leaders are in a fish bowl!

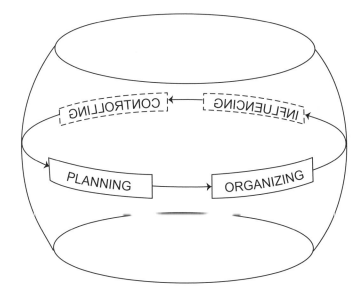

Figure 7.1: Cyclical and Interactive Management Functions

As leaders function within the fishbowl, they are fulfilling four important leadership functions. Even though many of these leadership functions are shared, leaders must accept the overall responsibility for the important functions of planning, organizing, influencing, and controlling. As depicted in Figure 7.1, these four cyclical, interactive leadership functions provide a conceptual framework for examining leadership and organizational effectiveness.

Leaders, regardless of desirability or preference, work in a "fish bowl" as illustrated in Figure 7.1. How leaders and members of their leadership teams fulfill the typical leadership functions of planning, organizing, influencing, and controlling will certainly impact the quality of the working environment and the productivity of the organization. These leadership functions are highly visible to key leaders throughout the system. However, these functions become less visible for individuals who are not directly involved in these leadership functions. Individuals throughout the organization **gain perceptions** about what is happening in the "fish bowl" through:

- their own personal experiences,
- their first-hand observations,
- insights from trusted friends and colleagues,
- informal conversations with colleagues,
- informal gossip sessions, and
- their own intuition.

Similar to viewing objects in a crazy mirror at a circus where the image bears little resemblance to reality, the image that others have of us and even the image that we have of ourselves may be governed by the reflection that we get from others about ourselves—what we think they think about us. Likewise in a fish bowl, individuals' external vantage point can magnify, diminish, and/or distort their view of reality. For example, if leaders have developed a reputation, justified or unjustified, that they are unwilling to share power with others, they will have difficulty in empowering others.

Another example that illustrates that *perceptions* of team members *are* their *reality* is based upon their responses to a **new** leader. If the "word gets out" from the former organization that the new leader **violates confidentiality,** the new leader will have difficulty overcoming this image. This will especially be true if the leader is unaware of this perception. The fact that they have heard and tentatively believe the leader misuses information clearly indicates that individuals will play it safe and not share important information. Therefore, open, honest two-way communications is negatively impacted.

The planning, organizing, influencing, and controlling processes are important leadership functions that can and need to be shared. As leaders increase the leadership capacity and incorporate the six leadership belief statements into their organizations, these leadership functions will be moved to the most appropriate level throughout their systems.

Planning

Effective leaders are skillful planners, and they are committed to helping other leaders develop effective planning skills and tools. Large and small units alike have numerous planning teams throughout their organizations.

For example, at the campus level, these teams may include but are not limited to:

- administrative teams,

- site-based teams,

- departments/grade level teams, and

- vertical teams.

Establishing and communicating a set of leadership beliefs regarding the parameters for quality decisions provide a solid foundation for these planning sessions. Knowing who should be involved in these deliberations is also crucial. Leaders who believe that decisions should be made as close to the point of implementation as possible will systematically involve the stakeholders in the planning process.

Organizing

Effective leaders are skillful organizers who involve stakeholders appropriately in this leadership function. They are sensitive to the needs of the individuals and groups and know when and how much to involve them. Believing that decisions should be made at the most appropriate level sends a clear message that there is a commitment to involve individuals who will be impacted by the decision in this leadership function. The formal leader and other key leaders need to possess or develop conceptual skills that enable them to organize human and financial resources to accomplish the specific goals and objectives.

Influencing

Leaders who involved stakeholders in the planning and organizing functions have also "built in" an influencing component. When leaders have appropriately involved individuals and groups within their work unit in the planning and organizing functions, their task of influencing the behavior of individuals and groups is relatively easy because of their initial involvement. The value of the initial involvement can be visually shown by the commitment gap vs. commitment level as shown in Figure 4.1. Individuals who were involved in the planning and organizing functions should be functioning primarily in Stages 5 and 6. They will be advocates and will be instrumental in helping members of their teams fulfill these expectations.

In utilizing the talents of independent team members in the planning and organizing functions, leaders are also increasing the "influence potential" throughout their units. Leaders who involve interdependent teams in these processes will find it easier to function as an ambassador to span organizational boundaries and influence external interdependent teams over which they have no legitimate power.

Controlling

The term "controlling" may carry some negative connotations, but it is still a very important leadership function. Organizations that do not have adequate controls built into their system are described as "out of control," "organizations in crisis," or "organizations that have lost their vision." The "controlling function" simply means that these organizations have a system in place that establishes a quality control standard. Ideally, these internal controls will be a function of interdependent teams whereby team members will hold each other and the team accountable. However, team leaders and members must know that leaders up line will reinforce the need for quality. This "dynamic tension" should be the result of granting professional autonomy and developing interdependence counterbalanced with organizational accountability. Even interdependent teams recognize the responsibility of leaders at the top of the organization to hold everyone accountable.

When teams initiate a new plan, organize it, and influence the behavior of groups and individuals, they should be able to have "predictability of behavior" or be able to control the outcomes. The basic purpose of the controlling function is to assist individuals and groups in achieving the goals that were established when the activity or event was initially planned. Based upon a set of unforeseen circumstances, there may be a need to reestablish different timelines or expectations.

These dynamic monitoring and adjusting activities are integral components of the controlling function. Similar to the auto-pilot computer function on airplanes that continuously self-corrects the aircraft to keep it on course, the "control function" in organizations is necessary to continuously monitor and maintain quality assurances, quality controls, and primary alignment with mission, vision, and values to keep the organization on course.

Feedback—the Breakfast of Champions

Leaders are highly visible as they work with members of their teams in planning, organizing, influencing, and controlling activities and events. Organizations need a systematic way of measuring their effectiveness. Effectiveness implies not only a focus on the product but also on the production capacity in the organization. Leaders should consider the wisdom of Aesop contained in the fable of *The Goose and The Golden Egg.* The care and feeding of the goose is essential to the continued production of golden eggs. Bottom line production, such as student achievement, is maintained and enhanced through careful and skillful provision, monitoring, and maintenance of mission critical resources. The resource most important to optimum production is the human resource. Consequently, a high priority for leaders is to attend to the perceived organizational health needs of the collective "goose."

To that end, the metaphor of functioning within a "fishbowl" seems very useful because it helps make an important distinction between the perceptions that individuals have and the reality as seen by the leader. As a leader functioning in the fishbowl, would it be helpful to have valid and reliable feedback about what "is" happening in your organization? Data, by definition, is value-neutral, and therefore should not be viewed as "good" or "bad." The *Organizational Health Instrument* is a valid and reliable diagnostic tool that will provide you with open and honest feedback. Percentile scores have been established for work units throughout educational organizations, to include elementary schools, middle schools, junior high schools, high schools, alternative schools, non-certified groups, central office units, the superintendency, school boards, and parents.

The Organizational Health Profile provides broad-based data to assist leaders in understanding the internal dynamics of their organizations. This feedback provides supporting data that may:

- clearly indicate the administrative unit is very healthy and, if needed, is capable of undergoing a major planned change effort successfully,

- indicate balance among the ten dimensions and reinforce current operating procedures,

- provide evidence that the leader and work unit members have a very similar view of the Organizational Health of the unit,

- provide evidence that there is a perceptual difference between the leader and work unit members (a line graph contrasts the leader's perception with that of work unit members), or

- provide evidence that there is an imbalance among the ten dimensions indicating that some organizational strengths may be contributing to an organizational improvement priority.

As leaders work in the "fish bowl" and accomplish these important leadership functions, their attitudes, knowledge, and communication and decision-making skills will greatly impact the organizational health of their unit.

The following are definitions of Organizational Health and the ten dimensions of Organizational Health:

Organizational Health is an organization's ability to function effectively, to cope adequately, to change appropriately, and to grow from within. This health can vary from a maximal to a minimal degree.

Goal Focus: Goal Focus is the ability of persons, groups, or organizations to have clarity, acceptance, support, and advocacy of goals and objectives.

Communication Adequacy: Communication Adequacy exists when information is relatively distortion free and travels both vertically and horizontally across the boundaries of an organization.

Optimal Power Equalization: Optimal Power Equalization is the ability to maintain a relatively equitable distribution of influence between leaders and team members.

Resource Utilization: Resource Utilization is the ability to coordinate and maintain inputs, particularly personnel, effectively with a minimal sense of strain.

Cohesiveness: Cohesiveness is the state when persons, groups, or organizations have a clear sense of identity. Members feel attracted to membership in an organization. They want to stay with it, be influenced by it, and exert their own influence within it.

Morale: Morale is that state in which a person, group, or organization has feelings of well-being, satisfaction, and pleasure.

Innovativeness: Innovativeness is that ability to be and allow others to be inventive, diverse, creative, and risk taking.

Autonomy: Autonomy is that state in which a person, group, or organization has the freedom to fulfill their roles and responsibilities.

Adaptation: Adaptation is that ability to tolerate stress and maintain stability while coping with demands of the environment.

Problem-solving Adequacy: Problem-solving Adequacy is an organization's ability to perceive problems and solve them with minimal energy. The problems stay solved and the problem-solving mechanism of the organization is maintained and/or strengthened.

Figure 7.2 is an actual profile of an organization and highlights the relationships among the ten dimensions of organizational health. The top strengths of the unit are:

- Resource Utilization,
- Goal Focus,
- Problem Solving Adequacy, and
- Communication Adequacy.

The two lowest dimensions are:

- Power and
- Morale.

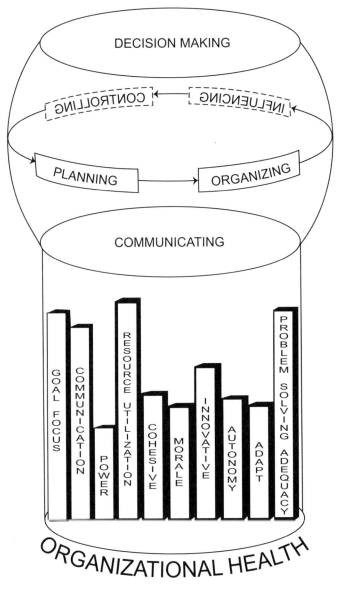

Figure 7.2: Functioning in the "Fish Bowl"

The contrast in levels of organizational health between Optimal Power Equalization and Resource Utilization has important implications for the leader and team members. High Resource Utilization clearly indicates that the leader knows and uses the talents of unit members. However, the relatively low score on Optimal Power Equalization indicates that members believe they do not have an opportunity to influence group or organization-wide decisions; and thus, they have a feeling of powerlessness. This sense of powerlessness can probably explain why Morale is relatively low. It is also clear that this is a well organized unit with relatively high Goal Focus and with systems in place for quality problem solving and effective communications.

The old adage, "What you don't know, can't hurt you" is not now—and never was—true. Operating in the "fish bowl" with limited data can be hazardous to your personal and Organizational Health. With diagnostic feedback from organizational members, the leader is in a position to capitalize on leadership and organizational strengths and to use those strengths to facilitate the designing of improvement strategies for a specific dimension. Using feedback from the system and subsystems should assist the leaders in improving the organization's health and effectiveness.

Data in the following chapter will clearly validate Matthew Miles' hypothesized relationship between Organizational Health and productivity. Miles' original conceptualization was that the dimensions of Organizational Health would:

- have a positive relationship to organizational productivity and

- help predict the results of a planned change effort.[5]

CHAPTER 8

THE RELATIONSHIP BETWEEN STUDENT PERFORMANCE AND ORGANIZATIONAL HEALTH

During the past twenty years of research, the Organizational Health Diagnostic and Development Corporation (OHDDC) has repeatedly and consistently found a strong relationship between Organizational Health and productivity. These data clearly show that keeping an organization "healthy" is going to enhance its potential for being productive and for becoming more productive. Leaders who want to establish and maintain a healthy and productive organizational environment have used these data to identify leadership and organizational strengths and improvement priorities.

Recently, a superintendent of schools requested a report examining the relationship between the ten dimensions of Organizational Health and the district student performance data. The first task was to identify and analyze all of the student performance data that had been generated by the state's accountability system.

This particular state used five batteries of tests in the elementary schools and six batteries of tests middle schools. Based on these **statewide assessment data,** the percent of students who scored at or above proficiency on each of these batteries of tests was identified at the state level and reported to the district.

For the elementary schools, the assessments consisted of third through fifth grade reading and fourth through fifth grade writing. Based on the percent of students who scored at or above proficiency in the five content areas, a **performance index** was established for each elementary school by computing the average proficiency for these five areas.

Likewise, a performance index was established for each middle school by identifying the percent of students who scored at or above proficiency on the battery of tests that constituted the state's accountability system. For the middle schools, the assessments consisted of sixth through eighth grade reading, seventh grade writing, and eighth grade math and science. Based on the percent of students who tested at or above proficiency in the six content areas, a **performance index** was established for each middle school by computing the average proficiency for these six content areas.

Since the Performance Index Score was going to be the unit of analysis, this score was entered into a spreadsheet along with each school's name, confidential code number established by the researcher, and the eleven sets of Organizational Health data. The following abbreviations and Organizational Health dimensions are listed below:

- GF   Goal Focus
- COM   Communication Adequacy
- OPE   Optimal Power Equalization
- RES   Resource Utilization
- COH   Cohesiveness
- MOR   Morale

- INN   Innovativeness
- AUT   Autonomy
- ADA   Adaptation
- PSA   Problem Solving Adequacy
- TOTAL   Composite Scores

The eighth character in the code numbers is the design-nation for type of schools: "E" for Elementary and "M" for Middle Schools. After the Performance Index Score was established for each school, no distinctions were made between elementary and middle schools. To prepare the data for this table and for the analysis, the researcher:

- Sorted the data from high to low based on the Performance Index Score for each school.

- Created a new column to record the ranking of schools from 1 to 30, with 1 representing the top performing school and 30 representing the school with the lowest Performance Index.

- Validated the accuracy of the newly created Performance Index Score by sending a summary of the raw data and the statistical analysis to the district's research department.

- Removed the names of the schools in order to provide for confidentiality.

- Placed these thirty schools into logical statistical groups based on the Performance Index Score:
    o Schools at or above the 75th percentile - Quadrant 4 (Q – 4),
    o Schools between 51st and 74th percentiles - Quadrant 3 (Q – 3),

    o   Schools between 26th and 50th percentiles - Quadrant 2 (Q – 2), and

    o   (Since no school had scores below 25th percentile, the schools were grouped into three rather than four groups.)

- Computed mean scores for the ten dimensions of Organizational Health and for the Total Organizational Health Score for these three levels of student performance.

As Table 8.1 depicts, the Performance Index Scores range from 77.3 to 35.6. Three schools are in Q-4, eighteen in Q-3, and nine in Q-2. Composite scores for each of the Organizational Health dimensions are also reported in Table 8.1.

The composite data from Table 8.1 are presented graphically in Figure 8.1. This Figure reveals that Q-4 schools had higher scores on all ten dimensions than those schools in Q-3 and Q-2. Q-3 schools had higher scores on eight of the ten dimensions than those schools in Q-2. This "stair step" relationship among these three groups of schools for eight of the ten dimensions highlights the importance of these Organizational Health dimensions and their impact upon student performance.

The dimensions that show the greatest variance between the top and bottom group and have the greatest impact upon student performance are:

- Goal Focus – The composite Goal Focus score for the top performing schools was 41 points higher than the Q-2 schools and 34 points higher than Q-3 schools.

NO.	PI	GF	COM	OPE	RES	COH	MOR	INN	AUT	ADA	PSA	TOTAL
				ORGANIZATIONAL HEALTH SCORES								
12E	77.3%	95%	66%	97%	91%	84%	79%	96%	96%	88%	52%	84%
29M	75.2%	85%	54%	63%	55%	14%	32%	53%	69%	55%	40%	52%
10E	75.0%	79%	73%	82%	83%	75%	75%	63%	81%	74%	83%	77%
Q4	Total	86%	64%	81%	76%	58%	62%	71%	82%	72%	58%	71%
20E	69.2%	88%	70%	93%	88%	81%	83%	98%	90%	87%	82%	86%
02E	67.2%	17%	17%	33%	41%	43%	30%	64%	50%	48%	17%	36%
22E	67.0%	67%	91%	94%	92%	87%	88%	93%	92%	83%	90%	88%
17E	66.8%	87%	96%	95%	92%	93%	89%	89%	99%	86%	96%	92%
01E	65.6%	42%	29%	50%	51%	30%	28%	45%	46%	31%	30%	38%
19E	64.0%	69%	75%	40%	74%	69%	71%	60%	57%	54%	74%	64%
21E	62.4%	16%	20%	12%	20%	41%	12%	24%	10%	40%	7%	20%
30M	60.7%	59%	63%	70%	61%	45%	66%	47%	71%	55%	59%	60%
14E	60.4%	34%	31%	26%	49%	14%	26%	60%	53%	50%	21%	36%
23M	57.8%	81%	89%	95%	83%	91%	86%	88%	80%	55%	83%	83%
25M	57.5%	88%	92%	92%	86%	70%	89%	81%	93%	78%	87%	86%
07E	55.2%	13%	13%	9%	17%	17%	8%	22%	15%	13%	5%	13%
08E	54.6%	41%	54%	64%	52%	30%	54%	32%	69%	35%	40%	47%
11E	53.8%	24%	11%	31%	12%	16%	31%	14%	28%	13%	7%	19%
18E	53.8%	55%	76%	73%	69%	62%	76%	67%	75%	54%	67%	67%
15E	53.0%	42%	48%	58%	47%	19%	33%	54%	65%	49%	28%	44%
24M	52.8%	66%	60%	77%	50%	40%	67%	52%	53%	40%	61%	57%
28M	51.5%	40%	32%	28%	45%	45%	34%	46%	29%	34%	40%	37%
Q3	Total	52%	54%	58%	57%	50%	54%	58%	60%	50%	50%	54%
03E	45.4%	25%	38%	76%	46%	15%	43%	28%	55%	18%	34%	38%
26M	43.5%	62%	83%	76%	81%	72%	76%	85%	66%	49%	69%	72%
06E	43.2%	38%	25%	54%	22%	28%	41%	39%	33%	26%	24%	33%
27M	41.8%	29%	51%	64%	44%	34%	53%	47%	45%	35%	38%	44%
13E	41.4%	22%	21%	26%	22%	15%	29%	55%	30%	13%	12%	25%
05E	40.6%	70%	45%	68%	83%	32%	63%	88%	66%	65%	34%	61%
09E	37.2%	81%	86%	85%	93%	71%	87%	94%	81%	73%	69%	82%
16E	37.2%	61%	56%	79%	62%	55%	49%	74%	39%	55%	63%	59%
04E	35.6%	13%	35%	38%	44%	11%	27%	40%	25%	13%	21%	27%
Q2	Total	45%	49%	63%	55%	37%	52%	61%	49%	39%	40%	49%

NO. = Code Number	PI = Performance Index

Table 8.1: Organizational Health and Student Performance

- Cohesiveness – The composite Cohesiveness score for Q-4 schools was 21 points higher than Q-2 schools and 8 points higher than Q-3 schools.

- Adaptation – The composite Adaptation score for Q-4 schools was 33 points higher than Q-2 schools and 22 points higher than Q-3 schools.

- Autonomy – The composite Autonomy score for the schools performing in Q-4 was 33 points higher than the scores for those schools having a Performance Index Score in Q-2 and 22 points higher than those in Q-3.

These data clearly show that:

- The degree to which faculties have clarity, acceptance, support, and advocacy of school-wide goals has a predictable influence on levels of student performance.

- The degree to which the faculties want to be a part of their work unit, want to influence each other, and are willing to be influenced by their peers has a predictable influence on the levels of student performance.

- The degree to which faculties are able to adapt and change to meet the demands from the external environment has a predictable influence on the levels of student performance.

- The degree to which faculties have been granted Autonomy to fulfill their professional role within the context of school-wide goals has a predictable influence on the levels of student performance.

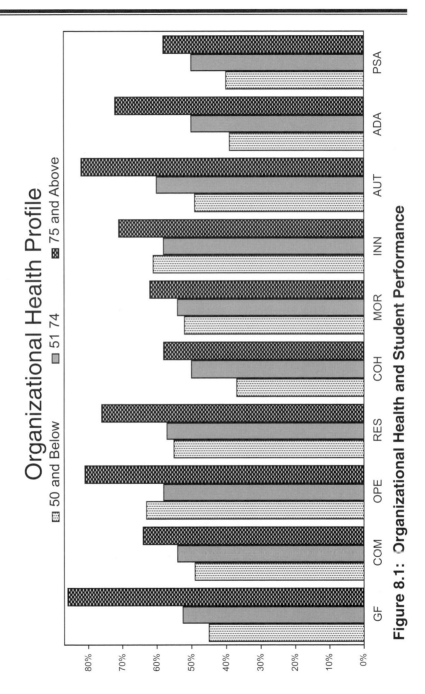

Figure 8.1: Organizational Health and Student Performance

To sharpen the focus on each of these ten dimensions and their relationship to these student performance data, each of the ten dimensions will be addressed in the following ten figures.

GOAL FOCUS AND STUDENT PERFORMANCE

Figure 8.2 highlights the relationship between Goal Focus and Student Performance. These data clearly indicate that the degree to which the faculty has clarity, acceptance, support, and advocacy for school-wide goals is related to the level of student performance.   These data highlight the importance of Goal Focus because:

- A strong commitment to goals translates into corresponding higher levels of student performance as reflected by the composite 86th percentile score on Goal Focus for Q-4 schools. At the advocacy level, team members are part of the quality control and quality assurance system because they are willing to hold each other accountable and responsible for results.

- A moderate level of support for goals can be expected to produce low to moderate results. The composite Goal Focus score for the Q-3 group was at the 52nd percentile, indicating that the commitment level was "very average."

- Likewise, a lack of clarity or support for school-wide goals will produce sporadic results at best. This may be caused by not having relevant goals, having too many goals, having goals only for the purpose of meeting local and state requirements, or having unresolved debates over the goals and/or disagreements about what needs to be done to accomplish the goals.

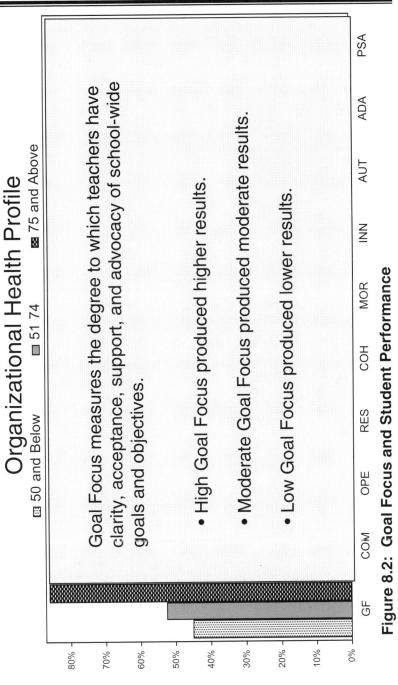

Organizational Health Profile

☷ 50 and Below   ■ 51 74   ▨ 75 and Above

Goal Focus measures the degree to which teachers have clarity, acceptance, support, and advocacy of school-wide goals and objectives.

- High Goal Focus produced higher results.
- Moderate Goal Focus produced moderate results.
- Low Goal Focus produced lower results.

Figure 8.2: Goal Focus and Student Performance

COMMUNICATION ADEQUACY AND STUDENT PERFORMANCE

The relationship between Communication Adequacy and Student Performance is highlighted by the data in Figure 8.3. These data, like the Goal Focus data, highlight a distinctive pattern among these three groups of schools and document a positive relationship between the levels of student performance and Communication Adequacy. Because these data clearly suggest that improved communications translates to improved productivity, principals and other school leaders have the opportunity and the obligation to improve the open, honest, two-way communications throughout their units.

Communication has deep significance for organizations since individuals make contributions to the achievement of organizational goals through personal and organizational communications systems. The degree and quality of goal focus, resource utilization, cohesiveness, adaptation, and problem-solving adequacy are at least partly a function of the quality of communication. More broadly, effective communication is:

- central to any productive interaction of people,

- the basis of cooperative effort, interpersonal influence, goal determination, and achievement of human and organizational growth,

- the process by which people are tied together in a work group,

- the bridge over which all technical knowledge and human relationships must travel, and

- the glue that holds organizations together, the very essence of an organization.

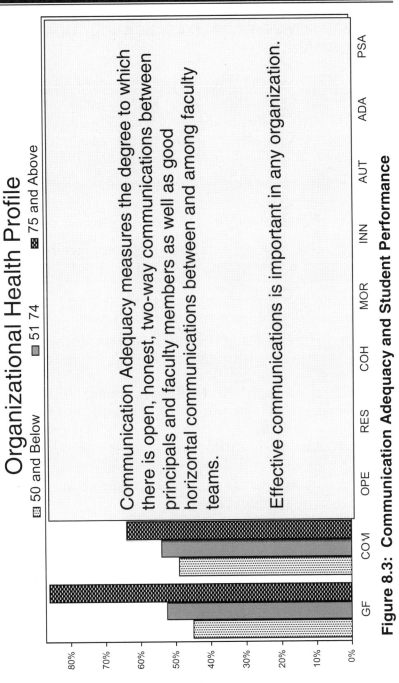

Organizational Health Profile

Communication Adequacy measures the degree to which there is open, honest, two-way communications between principals and faculty members as well as good horizontal communications between and among faculty teams.

Effective communications is important in any organization.

Figure 8.3: Communication Adequacy and Student Performance

OPTIMAL POWER EQUALIZATION AND STUDENT PERFORMANCE

Figure 8.4 presents the relationship between Optimal Power Equalization and Student Performance. Note that the "stair step" pattern does not exist for this dimension because the Q-2 schools have higher scores on Power Equalization than the Q-3 schools. Also note that:

- The number one Organizational Health strength for the Q2 schools was Optimal Power Equalization.

- The Q-4 schools had high empowerment (81) but higher scores on Goal Focus (86).

- The Q-3 schools score on empowerment was six points higher than Goal Focus.

- The Q-2 schools score on empowerment was 18 points higher than Goal Focus.

As reflected in Figure 3.1, the Empowerment Model, and in Leadership Belief Statement #3, leaders need to help individuals and teams move through the stages of development from dependent to independent to interdependence. Empowering dependent and independent teams prematurely can have a negative impact upon Goal Focus and productivity.

One could hypothesize that many of the individuals and teams within the Q-2 schools had been **empowered** to fulfill the mission and goals of the school without adequate school-wide focus, sufficient structures, and adequate support from above. Individuals and teams can perceive such inappropriate delegation of power as an abdication of responsibility by leaders.

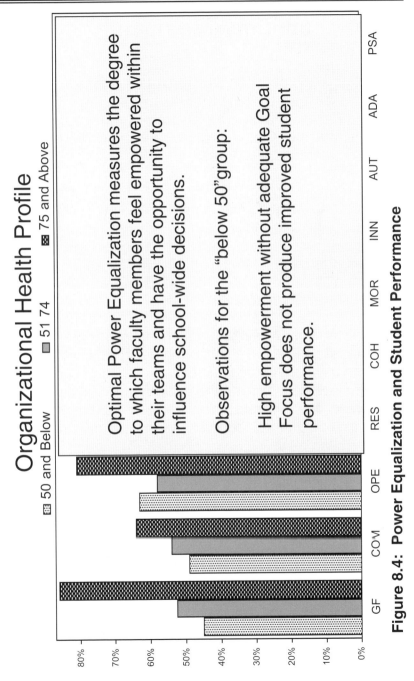

Figure 8.4: Power Equalization and Student Performance

127

RESOURCE UTILIZATON AND STUDENT PERFORMANCE

The relationship between Resource Utilization and Student Performance is highlighted by the data in Figure 8.5. These data, like the Goal Focus and Communication data, highlight the fact that a distinctive pattern exists among these three groups of schools.

As reflected in Figure 8.5, Resource Utilization measures the degree to which faculty members believe leaders know and are utilizing the human talents of individuals throughout the school. Tapping into these human resources throughout the school has great potential for increasing the leadership capacity of schools beyond members' traditional roles.

Productivity is maintained and enhanced through careful and skillful provision, monitoring, and maintenance of mission critical resources. The resource most important to optimum production is the human resource, as is highlighted by the fact that a major portion of every school's operational budget is expended on human resources.

Therefore, leaders need to capitalize on their human resources in order to increase productivity, remembering the lesson from Aesop that the "care and feeding of the goose" is essential to the continued production of golden eggs.

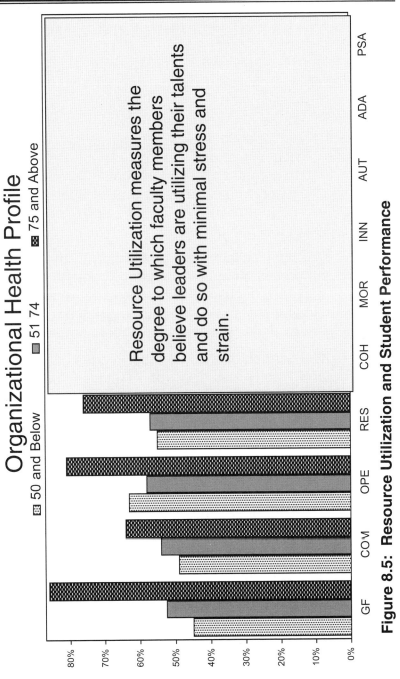

Figure 8.5: Resource Utilization and Student Performance

COHESIVENESS AND STUDENT PERFORMANCE

The relationship between Cohesiveness and Student Performance is highlighted by the data in Figure 8.6 and shows a distinctive and predictable pattern. Cohesiveness measures the degree to which individuals and teams work well as independent and interdependent teams to accomplish the goals of the school. These data clearly indicate that the trust and support that individuals have within and between teams have an impact upon the level of student performance. Based upon the team development model in Figure 4.1:

- The Q-4 schools are performing in the "getting organized" stage of team development. Because they are focusing their collective energies on "finding solutions" rather than "finding fault," they are focused on increasing student performance.

- Q-3 schools are in the latter stages of Infighting and early stages of Getting Organized. Therefore, it is understandable that their performance scores are higher than the Q-2 schools and lower than the Q-4 schools.

- The Q-2 schools are "locked into" the Infighting stage of Team Development. The amount of energy expended over unresolved issues detracts from the team effort needed to accomplish school-wide goals. Individuals and teams in the Q-2 schools have been empowered to a high degree, which allows them to function independently and contributes to the infighting and low cohesiveness.

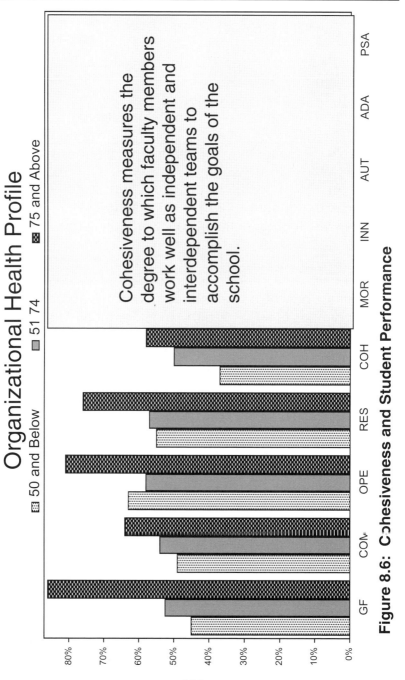

Organizational Health Profile

▦ 50 and Below ▥ 51 74 ▨ 75 and Above

Cohesiveness measures the degree to which faculty members work well as independent and interdependent teams to accomplish the goals of the school.

Figure 8.6: Cohesiveness and Student Performance

MORALE AND STUDENT PERFORMANCE

The relationship between Morale and Student Performance is highlighted by the data in Figure 8.7. These data, like five of the six previous dimensions have the "stair step" relationship between the Organizational Health dimension and Student Performance. However, the range of scores for Morale is smaller than the other nine dimensions.

Morale is the most elusive of the ten dimensions. It measures the degree to which individuals have a sense of security, well-being, satisfaction, and pleasure. Morale may be the most interdependent dimension because when morale is relatively low, one can predict that at least one of the other dimensions is also negatively impacting morale. The dimensions of power equalization and autonomy are the two dimensions that are the most frequently associated with low morale. When morale is low, leaders typically find that individuals and teams are not productive. When morale is high, leaders can expect that individuals and teams are willing and able to innovatively participate in the decision-making and problem-solving processes.

These data clearly indicate that for these thirty schools Morale doesn't have the level of impact on student performance as do seven of the other dimensions. Therefore, high empowerment without adequate focus, structures, and systems may result a general state of workplace happiness but not result in high performance.

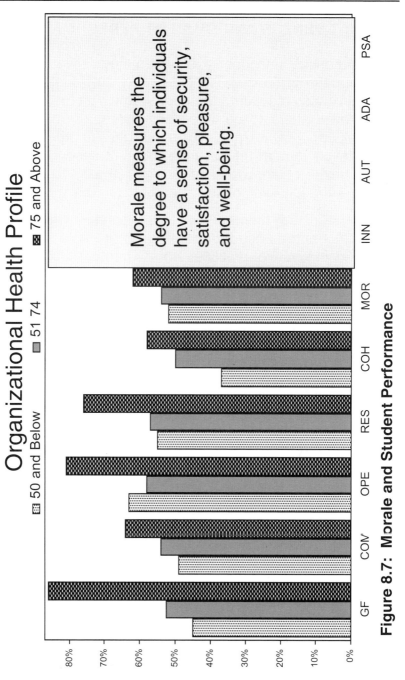

Figure 8.7: Morale and Student Performance

INNOVATIVENESS AND STUDENT PERFORMANCE

The interesting relationship between Innovativeness and Student Performance is presented in Figure 8.8. Innovativeness measures the degree to which the leader is and allows others to be inventive, diverse, creative, and risk taking. This pattern is similar to the Power Equalization dimension because the Q-2 schools have a higher level of Innovativeness than the Q-3 schools. Consider the following observations:

- Faculty members in those schools that had a Performance Index below 50 are able to initiate innovative practices to a greater degree than their Q-3 counterparts and are within ten percentage points of the Q-4 schools.

- In the Q-4 schools, Goal Focus was 15 points higher than Innovativeness.

- In the Q-3 schools, Goal Focus was six points lower than Innovativeness.

- In Q-2 schools, Goal Focus was 16 points lower than Innovativeness.

These student performance data clearly suggest that Innovativeness should take place within the context of the school-wide goals and priorities.

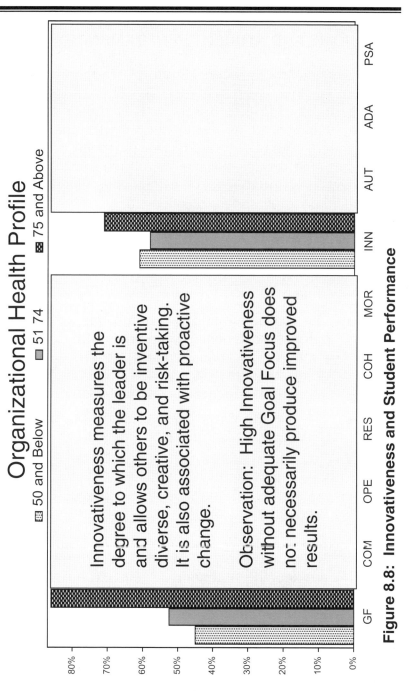

Organizational Health Profile

Legend: 50 and Below | 51 74 | 75 and Above

Innovativeness measures the degree to which the leader is and allows others to be inventive diverse, creative, and risk-taking. It is also associated with proactive change.

Observation: High Innovativeness without adequate Goal Focus does not necessarily produce improved results.

Categories: GF, COM, OPE, RES, COH, MOR, INN, AUT, ADA, PSA

Figure 8.8: Innovativeness and Student Performance

AUTONOMY AND STUDENT PERFORMANCE

The relationship between Student Performance and Autonomy within the parameters of team and campus goals is depicted in Figure 8.9. This is a very distinctive pattern that coincides with the levels of student performance. Autonomy measures the degree to which individuals and groups believe they have the freedom to make decisions and to function within what they believe is, and should be, their sphere of influence.

This figure shows a healthier relationship between Goal Focus and Autonomy than was present with Power Equalization and Innovativeness. This Goal Focus and Autonomy data reveal the following relationships:

- The top performing Q-4 group has an excellent balance between Autonomy (82) and Goal Focus (86). These leaders are in a position to grant autonomy because of individual and team support and advocacy of school-wide goals.

- The middle Q-3 group also has a relatively good balance between the two dimensions. Because Autonomy (60) is higher than Goal Focus (52), the implication is that since there is less advocacy for goals, leaders should grant less Autonomy.

- The balance for the lowest performing Q-2 group is also relatively good. Note that these leaders are keeping Autonomy in balance but are failing to do so with Power Equalization and Innovativeness. This may also suggest that some of the Autonomy issues are being impacted by the district or state.

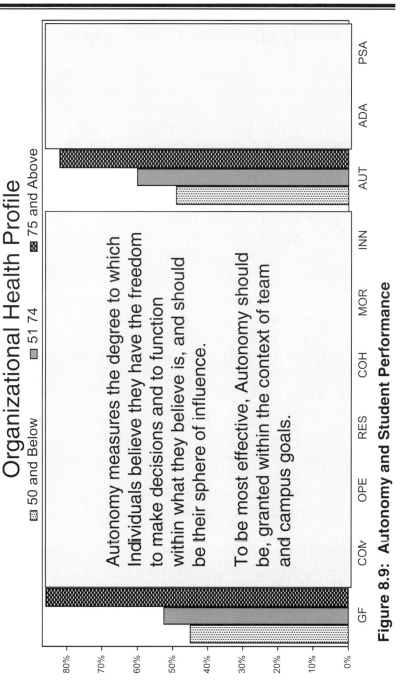

Organizational Health Profile

☷ 50 and Below   ▪ 51 74   ▦ 75 and Above

Autonomy measures the degree to which Individuals believe they have the freedom to make decisions and to function within what they believe is, and should be their sphere of influence.

To be most effective, Autonomy should be, granted within the context of team and campus goals.

Figure 8.9: Autonomy and Student Performance

ADAPTATION AND STUDENT PERFORMANCE

The relationship between Student Performance and Adaptation is depicted in Figure 8.10 and shows a very distinctive pattern that coincides with the levels of student performance. As our data has consistently demonstrated, Adaptation highly correlates with student performance. Adaptation measures the degree to which members believe their school is able to adapt and change to meet the unique needs of their students within the context of school goals and personal belief systems. Consider the following response options to external pressures for change. When challenged to increase the level of student performance:

- Many teachers in low performing schools can be expected to say, "The majority of my students are low SES, highly mobile, English as second language, with low or no parent involvement, etc. **Therefore,** I just can't meet those goals with these students."

- Many teachers in high performing schools can be expected to say, "The majority of my students are low SES, highly mobile, English as second language, with low or no parent involvement, etc. **Therefore,** we must change and compensate for these factors, whatever it takes."

The critical issue is what comes after the **"therefore."** Professionals in high performing schools view these conditions as mandates for adaptation rather than as built in excuses to avoid accepting responsibility.

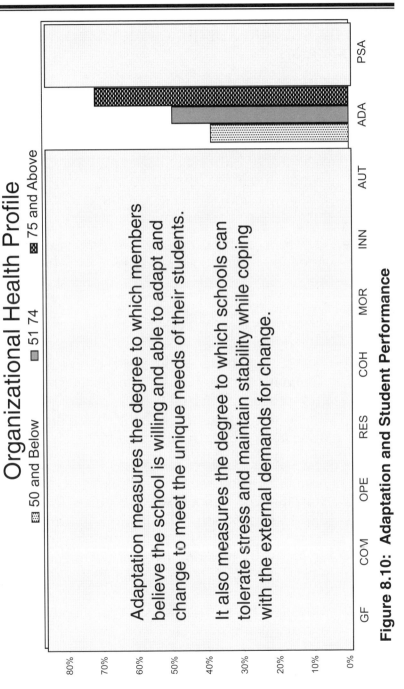

Figure 8.10: Adaptation and Student Performance

PROBLEM SOLVING ADEQUACY AND STUDENT PERFORMANCE

Problem Solving measures the degree to which the school is able to perceive and solve problems with minimal energy. Figure 8.11 presents the relationship between Student Performance and Problem Solving Adequacy, again depicting the "stair step" pattern. Although the spread between the three groups is less than for Goal Focus, Autonomy, and Adaptation, these data clearly reinforce the need for adequate problem solving:

- Q-4 schools have a composite Problem Solving Adequacy percentile score of 71. When the day-to-day problems get solved and stay solved in an efficient and effective manner, teachers have more time and energy to focus on the real purpose of schools – student learning for all.

- Q-3 schools have a composite Problem Solving Adequacy score of 54—17 points lower than the Q-4 schools. As they expend energy on the day-to-day issues without problem-solving adequacy, they have less time for teaching.

- Q-2 schools have a composite Problem Solving Adequacy score of 41, which is 25 points lower than the Q-4 schools and 13 points lower than the Q-3 schools. Their Power Equalization scores suggest that their leaders have entrusted them with making decisions independently, which can place them in win/lose or lose/win positions when their decisions are not being mediated by the leader. Consequently, issues and problems may be "swept under the carpet" and remain unresolved.

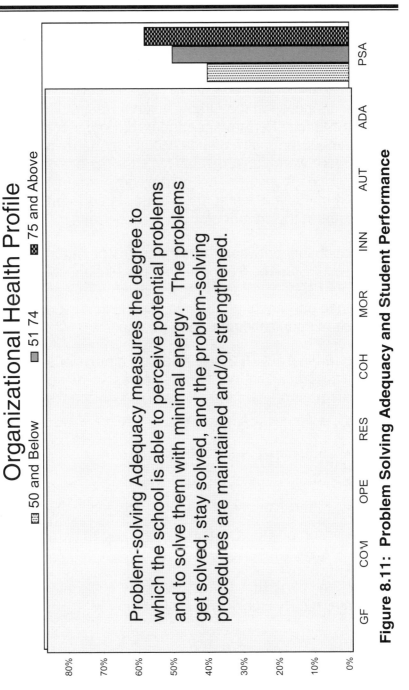

Organizational Health Profile

□ 50 and Below   ■ 51 74   ⊠ 75 and Above

Problem-solving Adequacy measures the degree to which the school is able to perceive potential problems and to solve them with minimal energy. The problems get solved, stay solved, and the problem-solving procedures are maintained and/or strengthened.

GF   COM   OPE   RES   COH   MOR   INN   AUT   ADA   PSA

80%
70%
60%
50%
40%
30%
20%
10%
0%

Figure 8.11: Problem Solving Adequacy and Student Performance

ORGANIZATIONAL HEALTH DIMENSIONS AND THE PERFORMANCE INDEX

The data in Table 8.2 were prepared to show the relationship between the Organizational Health dimensions and the Student Performance Index. In order to assign a code number that corresponds with the performance level, the schools were ranked from high to low based on the Performance Index. These rankings from 1-30 are recorded in column 3 and are used as a code number for the schools in the scatter plots.

The relationship between the dimensions of Organizational Health and Student Performance correlation coefficients were computed, and levels of statistical significance were determined for each of the ten dimensions and for the composite Organizational Health Scores.

As reported in Table 8.2, the following dimensions and the composite Organizational Health scores were statistically significant at or beyond the .05 level of significance:

- Adaptation at the .01 level,

- Autonomy at the .01 level,

- Goal Focus at the .05 level,

- Cohesiveness at the .05 level, and

- Composite Organizational Health at the .05 level.

The scatter plots that follow will show a visual image of these statistically significant relationships.

NO.	PI	PC	Organizational Health Scores										
			GF	COM	OPE	RES	COH	MOR	INN	AUT	ADA	PSA	Total
12E	77.3%	1	95%	66%	97%	91%	84%	79%	96%	96%	88%	52%	84%
29M	75.2%	2	85%	54%	63%	55%	14%	32%	53%	69%	55%	40%	52%
10E	75.0%	3	79%	73%	82%	83%	75%	75%	63%	81%	74%	83%	77%
20E	69.2%	4	88%	70%	93%	88%	81%	83%	98%	90%	87%	82%	86%
02E	67.2%	5	17%	17%	33%	41%	43%	30%	64%	50%	48%	17%	36%
22E	67.0%	6	67%	91%	94%	92%	87%	88%	93%	92%	83%	90%	88%
17E	66.8%	7	87%	96%	95%	92%	93%	89%	89%	99%	86%	96%	92%
01E	65.6%	8	42%	29%	50%	51%	30%	28%	45%	46%	31%	30%	38%
19E	64.0%	9	69%	75%	40%	74%	69%	71%	60%	57%	54%	74%	64%
21E	62.4%	10	16%	20%	12%	20%	41%	12%	24%	10%	40%	7%	20%
30M	60.7%	11	59%	63%	70%	61%	45%	66%	47%	71%	55%	59%	60%
14E	60.4%	12	34%	31%	26%	49%	14%	26%	60%	53%	50%	21%	36%
23M	57.8%	13	81%	89%	95%	83%	91%	86%	88%	80%	55%	83%	83%
25M	57.5%	14	88%	92%	92%	86%	70%	89%	81%	93%	78%	87%	86%
07E	55.2%	15	13%	13%	9%	17%	17%	8%	22%	15%	13%	5%	13%
08E	54.6%	16	41%	54%	64%	52%	30%	54%	32%	69%	35%	40%	47%
11E	53.8%	17	24%	11%	31%	12%	16%	31%	14%	28%	13%	7%	19%
18E	53.8%	18	55%	76%	73%	69%	62%	76%	67%	75%	54%	67%	67%
15E	53.0%	19	42%	48%	58%	47%	19%	33%	54%	65%	49%	28%	44%
24M	52.8%	20	66%	60%	77%	50%	40%	67%	52%	53%	40%	61%	57%
28M	51.5%	21	40%	32%	28%	45%	45%	34%	46%	29%	34%	40%	37%
03E	45.4%	22	25%	38%	76%	46%	15%	43%	28%	55%	18%	34%	38%
26M	43.5%	23	62%	83%	76%	81%	72%	76%	85%	66%	49%	69%	72%
06E	43.2%	24	38%	25%	54%	22%	28%	41%	39%	33%	26%	24%	33%
27M	41.8%	25	29%	51%	64%	44%	34%	53%	47%	45%	35%	38%	44%
13E	41.4%	26	22%	21%	26%	22%	15%	29%	55%	30%	13%	12%	25%
05E	40.6%	27	70%	45%	68%	83%	32%	63%	88%	66%	65%	34%	61%
09E	37.2%	28	81%	86%	85%	93%	71%	87%	94%	81%	73%	69%	82%
16E	37.2%	29	61%	56%	79%	62%	55%	49%	74%	39%	55%	63%	59%
04E	35.6%	30	13%	35%	38%	44%	11%	27%	40%	25%	13%	21%	27%
C. Coefficient		0.39					0.36			0.43	0.50		0.32
Significance L.		0.05					0.05			0.01	0.01		0.05
PI = Performance Index							PC = Performance Code - Rank Order						

Table 8.2: Correlations between Student Performance and OH Dimensions

GOAL FOCUS AND THE PERFORMANCE INDEX

Figure 8.12 provides a visual image of the relationship between the faculty perception of Goal Focus and the school Performance Index with the performance Index plotted on the vertical axis and Goal Focus scores plotted on the horizontal axis. The symbols represent the rank order of the schools where Numbers 1 and 30 represent the top and bottom performing schools respectively.

As Table 8.2 shows, this relationship is statistically significant at the .05 level of significance. The diagonal lines above and below the correlation line represent deviations 25 percentile points above and below a perfect correlation. It is important to note that although some schools are outside this measure of deviation, the relationships are statistically significant.

The five schools above the top diagonal line and the three schools below the diagonal line are outliers. Students in the five schools (5, 10, 15, 17, & 12) above the diagonal line are performing at higher levels than anticipated, and the students in the three schools (28, 27, & 14) below the diagonal line are performing less well than anticipated.

What implications do these outliers have for key central office leaders? They could have important implications for organizational structures, roles and responsibilities, leadership and team development, skill development for leaders and team members, etc. These are invaluable data for leaders responsible for working collaboratively with these principals and faculties.

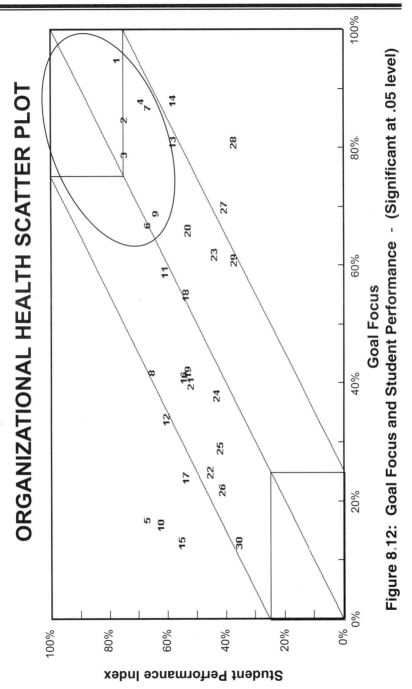

ORGANIZATIONAL HEALTH SCATTER PLOT

Figure 8.12: Goal Focus and Student Performance - (Significant at .05 level)

145

Initially, these data raise the following questions:

- What are some potential contributing factors that are causing students in these five schools to perform at higher levels than anticipated?
  - o Perhaps a change in top leadership caused the faculty to adopt a "wait and see posture" or to resist the direction of the leadership.
  - o Perhaps experienced faculties are committed to quality teaching within their grade levels or teams but do not see a school-wide leadership thrust.
  - o Perhaps students are performing well without high Goal Focus by key leaders due to strong parental influence.
- What factors are potentially causing students in the three schools with high levels of Goal Focus to perform less well than anticipated?
  - o The faculty may be highly committed to the goals but have a challenging population.
  - o The faculty may be highly committed but may need additional resources to improve student performance.
  - o The faculty may be committed to the goals, but existing goals may not include the need for vertical alignment.
  - o A new leader may have gained high focus but need more time to translate focus into higher performance.

ADAPTATION AND THE PERFORMANCE INDEX

The relationship between Student Performance and Adaptation is statistically significant beyond the .01 level of significance. These statistical data were reported in Table 8.2 and are graphically presented in Figure 8.13. Top performing schools as represented by their rankings on the Student Performance Index are predominantly within the identified circle: 1, 2, 3, 4, 5, 6, 7, 9, 11, 12, 13, 14, 18 and 19. These data clearly suggest that the levels of student performance can be increased by assisting schools in becoming more willing and able to adapt and make appropriate changes.

By critically analyzing the outliers in a similar way that was done with Goal Focus and Student Performance, district leaders and principals will be in a position to:

- Forecast and anticipate needed changes; thus, leaders will be able to involve members in planning the planned change effort.

- Explore factors that facilitate and inhibit schools, teams, and individuals during planned change efforts.

- Determine the influence that central office administrators and principals have on this change process.

  For example, if principals report back to their faculties and give "credit" to their supervisor for a significant change effort, these principals will be knowingly or unknowingly contributing to internal resistance to the idea by implying that "they made us do it."

147

Reactive, directive leaders can get desired results for expectations imposed from above, but the faculty perception may be one of "this too shall pass." They do not perceive a high level of organizational commitment to and capacity for adaptation.

Faculties in these schools may be responding to external change demand based on personal and professional need satisfaction but do not perceive the organization and its leaders as sharing that need.

Central office personnel may determine that their planning process should involve principals much earlier in the planned change efforts.

- Determine the cause of the resistance to change. It could be a result of one or more of the following:

    o Members do not see a need to change.

    o Members do not have the knowledge, skills, or confidence to successfully implement the change effort.

    o Members are unwilling to change because they lack confidence in the leader and system to support and sustain change efforts.

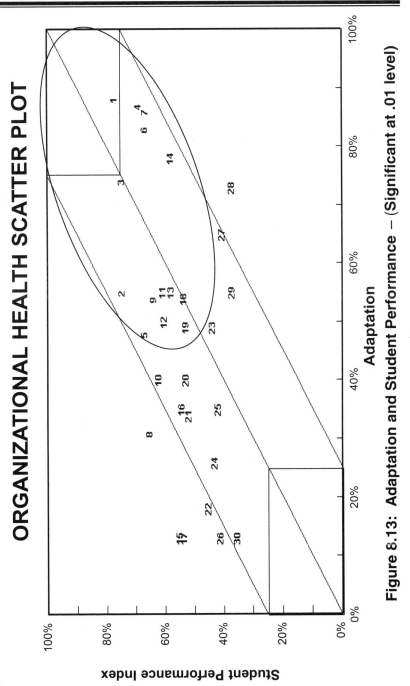

ORGANIZATIONAL HEALTH SCATTER PLOT

Figure 8.13: Adaptation and Student Performance – (Significant at .01 level)

COHESIVENESS AND THE PERFORMANCE INDEX

The relationship between Student Performance and Cohesiveness was statistically significant at the .05 level of significance. These statistical data were reported in Table 8.2 and are graphically presented in Figure 8.14. This scatter plot provides powerful evidence to central office leaders and principals that team efforts are crucial.

As presented in Figure 4.1, leaders need to be aware of and sensitive to the six stages of team development. All of the schools above the diagonal line except for school # 8 are also in Stage I in the Team Development Cycle. The prevailing norm for schools in Stage 1 is to "play it safe." It is not uncommon to hear individuals within Stage 1 to say, "I am going back to my classroom, close my door, teach my class, and I won't care what else happens!"

These data **suggest that leaders could have a significant impact upon student performance** by focusing their energies on helping individuals and teams progress through the six stages of development as presented in Figure 4.1 by:

- Providing for the security needs of team members and the structure necessary for encouraging and promoting individuals and teams to progress from Stage 1 to higher levels in the Team Development Cycle. Eight of these campuses are functioning in Stage 1 or Testing.

- Helping leaders and key members view differences of opinion and disagreements as natural and healthy and helping them work through these differences. Approaching these differences from a win/win perspective rather than win/lose is imperative. These differences of opinions create opportunities for releasing the synergy within groups and can propel the team into Stage 3.

- Creating a culture and expectation that teams will be able to function primarily in Stage 3 and above. In Stage 3 the leader will use a collaborative leadership style and help the group focus its energies on confronting issues rather than individuals, on establishing procedures for improving existing conditions, and for providing opportunities for team members to gain new knowledge and skills.

- Expecting and supporting individual teams to experience Stage 4, Mature Closeness as a team. Within these teams leadership is truly shared, and members of the team will feel comfortable initiating leadership acts, refocusing the group on issues, proposing improved ways of doing business, and assisting other team members in achieving quality.

- Creating the expectation that teams throughout the school will be able to function as Interdependent Teams in Stages 5. These teams will be encouraged to think and act interdependently, think conceptually, search for long-term win/win strategies, provide data-based feedback, and identify needs of the team so that new skills can be developed and additional resources provided.

- Providing the opportunity for interdependent teams to function in Stage 6 and to serve as ambassadors and work with other interdependent teams internal and external to the system.

It can be expected that interdependent teams will:

- hold themselves and others accountable for the highest standards of mission accomplishment,

- identify discrepancies between stakeholder needs and mission purposes,

- analyze causes for gaps between actual and desired results,

- predict future trends, and

- plan proactively.

As reflected in Figure 8.14, a majority of these schools were functioning primarily in Stages 1 and 2 in the Team Development Cycle. These data strongly suggest that performance data for these schools could be dramatically improved by focusing energies on helping individual teams move to higher levels in the Team Development Cycle.

In the past leaders may have had the luxury of allowing teachers to work independently as individuals and teams. However, in the arena of "high stakes" accountability, it is crucial that leaders capitalize on the talents of all individuals and help them function vertically and horizontally as interdependent teams.

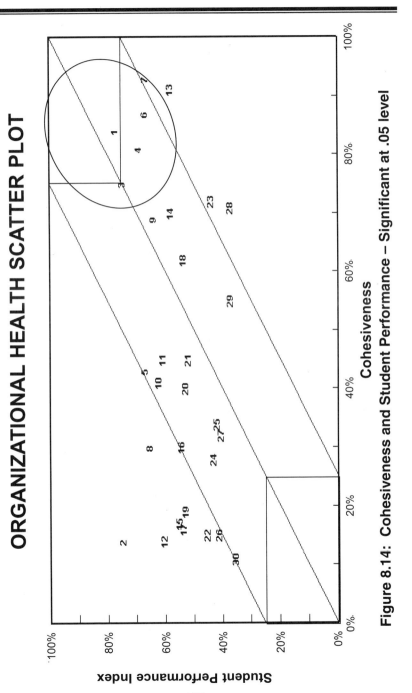

ORGANIZATIONAL HEALTH SCATTER PLOT

Figure 8.14: Cohesiveness and Student Performance – Significant at .05 level

153

AUTONOMY AND THE PERFORMANCE INDEX

The relationship between Student Performance and Autonomy was statistically significant at the .01 level of significance. These statistical data were reported in Table 8.2 and are graphically presented in Figure 8.15.

Even though this pattern produces a statistically significant relationship, six of the schools are considered to be outliers. The three schools above the top diagonal line and the three schools below the diagonal line are outliers. Students in the schools 10, 15, and 17 are above the diagonal line are performing at higher levels than one would have anticipated, and the students in schools 28, 14, and 7 below the diagonal line are performing less well than one would have anticipated.

Central office personnel and the six principals should be able to gain important insights regarding the internal workings of their schools. The data clearly suggest that the level of student performance should increase if:

- Leaders in schools 28, 14, and 7 would provide more structure and assistance to independent teams so they can function as interdependent teams. Leaders need to be actively involved helping these teams think interdependently.

- Leaders in schools 10, 15, and 17 would provide more autonomy to the individuals capable of independent and interdependent actions. These leaders may need to change their leadership styles/strategies because they appear to be in a power struggle with key faculty members and are being viewed as not trusting and trying to control everything. They may have misdiagnosed the needs and capacity of the faculty. These leaders may be assuming that these individuals are dependent and need close supervision; however, these individuals and teams may be or view themselves as individuals capable of independent and interdependent actions.

CONCLUSIONS

As reported in Table 8.2, the composite Organizational Health score and the dimensions of Goal Focus, Adaptation, Cohesiveness, and Autonomy were statistically significant. These results clearly reinforce Matthew Miles' early hypothesis that the Organizational Health levels will be a predictor of organizational productivity. Furthermore, these **statistically significant data** reinforce the interrelationships within and between our leadership belief statements and conceptual models. More specifically:

- Leadership Belief #1, as reflected by being placed in the center of the star in Figure 8, is the starting place for leaders who want to impact the focus and productivity of their organization. The belief statement provides the mission-driven parameters for achieving quality decisions.

- Leadership Beliefs #2 and #3 speak to the fact that moving the decision as close to the point of implementation is important, but leaders who empower individuals who do not have the expertise, skills, or motivation to make quality decisions is dysfunctional. Incorporating these two belief statements into the culture and day-to-day practice will facilitate proactive organizations to **adapt** to meet the ever-changing needs of their constituents.

155

Highly effective leaders who expect individuals to move through the empowerment continuum will be willing to facilitate individuals and teams to become **proactive adapters.** These research data also reinforce our belief that empowerment and problem solving must be done within the context of the school wide goals.

- Leadership Belief #4 focuses on the importance of recognizing and facilitating the movement of teams through the six stages of Team Development as depicted in Figure 4.1. The study reported above, as well as many previous studies, emphasizes that it takes a team effort to become and remain a highly productive and **cohesive** organization.

- Leadership Belief #5 emphasizes the importance of **Autonomy.** As evidenced by the study reported above, helping individuals and teams progress through the growth continuum from accountability to responsibility as shown in Figure 5.1 will positively impact organizational productivity.

- Leadership Belief #6 focuses on building in quality assurance and control strategies throughout the organization. Establishing feedback processes that give "voice to relevant data" is crucial for accomplishing this leadership belief statement and for incorporating the previous five leadership belief statements into the organizational culture.

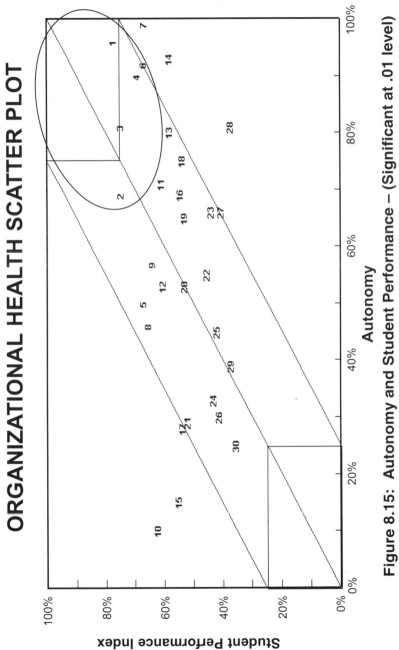

ORGANIZATIONAL HEALTH SCATTER PLOT

Figure 8.15: Autonomy and Student Performance – (Significant at .01 level)

157

Effective leaders view feedback data and its analysis as the "breakfast of champions." Because the Organizational Health Diagnostic and Development Corporation (OHDDC) has repeatedly and consistently found a strong relationship between Organizational Health and productivity over the past twenty years, many school district leaders have used our data to establish and maintain a healthy and productive organizational environment.

Further current information regarding the important relationship between organizational health and productivity is reported in our website at *www.organizationalhealth.com* in the section entitled **student performance.**

SUMMARY

We believe improving the Organizational Health and productivity is a critical function of leadership. It should be clear that:

- we are advocates for increasing the leadership capacity of individuals and teams throughout the organization, and

- we believe the role of the leader is absolutely central and crucial to that process.

Our support materials, ***Organizational Health: Improvement Strategies*** and each of the ten individual Organizational Health chapters, clearly acknowledge that leaders are the ones who are in the pivotal position to improve the Organizational Health and productivity of their organizations.

As established in our support materials mentioned previously, we believe that the Organizational Health and effectiveness of any organization can be significantly enhanced by any one or a combination of the following:

- Changing leadership behaviors,

- Changing the behaviors of individuals and teams within the organization,

- Changing the organizational structures within the administrative unit, and

- Helping individuals to understand the "whys" behind leader decisions and behaviors.

Incorporating our Leadership Belief Statements into the fabric of your organization can provide an infrastructure that clearly signals to individuals that you are committed to helping individuals and teams move from dependence, to independence, to interdependence.   By teaching these leadership models to members of your team, you are creating a common language and building a community of leaders who are able to think and act interdependently. Thus, performance and productivity can be expected to improve.

Our goal is to provide cost effective, diagnostic and development strategies to improve leadership and organizational effectiveness for schools and school systems of the 21st Century.

The objective of Organizational Health is to provide diagnostic and development materials for leaders who are data-based and who believe in developing the leadership of district administrators, principals, and faculty teams.

FOOTNOTES

1. Paul Hersey and Kenneth H. Blanchard, *Management of Organizational Behavior* (Englewood Cliffs, N.J.: Prentice-Hall, 1988), p. 287.

2. Stephen R. Covey, *The Seven Habits of Highly Effective People* (New York: Simon and Schuster, 1989), pp. 48-52.

3. Stephen R. Covey, *The 4 Roles of Leadership* (USA: Franklin Covey, 1999), pp. 166-175.

4. Peter F. Drucker, *Management Challenges for the 21st Century* (New York: HarperCollins, 1999) p. 8.

5. Matthew B. Miles, "Planned Change and Organizational Health: Figure and Ground," *Administering Human Resources*, Francis M. Trusty, ed. (Berkeley: McCutchan Publishing Company, 1971), pp. 335-345.

APPENDIX A

Please circle the response that most closely reflects your perception regarding these issues where O = Out of alignment, P = Partial Alignment, E = Excellent Alignment, and U = Unsure:

	Right Mission				
1.	To what extent is the organization's mission aligned with the needs of current and future stakeholders?	O	P	E	U
2.	To what extent are our mission, vision, and values aligned with the expectation of "Learning for all, whatever it takes?"	O	P	E	U
3.	To what extent is the organization's mission aligned with my personal mission?	O	P	E	U
4.	To what extent are my job responsibilities aligned with the organization's mission?	O	P	E	U
	Right People				
5.	To what extent are our personnel policies, procedures, and actual practices aligned to insure that the right people are employed	O	P	E	U
6.	To what extent are our personnel policies, procedures, and actual practices aligned to insure that the right people are retained and developed?	O	P	E	U
7.	To what extent are our personnel policies, procedures, and actual practices aligned to promote job enlargement opportunities?	O	P	E	U
	Right Structures				
8.	To what extent are our roles and responsibilities aligned with our goals?	O	P	E	U
9.	To what extent are rules and regulations aligned with our goals?	O	P	E	U
10.	To what extent is our curriculum vertically aligned?	O	P	E	U
11.	To what extent do the structures encourage alignment across content areas? (In other words, is your content contained in isolated silos or integrated across disciplines?)	O	P	E	U

12.	To what extent are resources such as technology aligned with our priorities? (In other words, are resources assigned on a need basis or on a personal basis?)	O	P	E	U
13.	To what extent are the agenda for organizational meetings aligned with our goals?	O	P	E	U
14.	To what extent do our structures support our tasks? (Is there an appropriate mix between command and control structure and team structure?)	O	P	E	U
15	To what extent is what we **say** aligned with what we **do**?	O	P	E	U
	Right Processes				
16.	To what extent are our vertical leadership teams' decisions aligned with our commitment to shared interdependent decision-making?	O	P	E	U
17.	To what extent are our horizontal teams' decisions aligned with our commitment to shared interdependent decision-making?	O	P	E	U
18.	To what extent do our leadership teams above align feedback with technological capacity? (In other words, are they using technology-based strategies such as email, list-servs, intra-web networks, chat-rooms, etc. for feedback purposes?)	O	P	E	U
19.	To what extent are the decisions and deliberations made in staff meetings aligned with stakeholder priorities?	O	P	E	U
20.	To what extent are information technologies inside the organization aligned with information technologies outside the organization?	O	P	E	U
	Right Information				
21.	To what extent is access to relevant information aligned with the needs of decision-makers?	O	P	E	U
22.	To what extent is there alignment between the authority to make decisions and access to relevant and accurate data?	O	P	E	U

23.	To what extent is there alignment between the practice of open, honest information sharing and the need for confidentiality of private/sensitive information?	O	P	E	U
24.	To what extent is there alignment between the important practice of reporting minutes from official meetings and the need for open, honest but private dialogue? (For example, are minutes of official meetings restricted only to a record of actions taken or do they include a reporting of "Who said what about whom"?)	O	P	E	U
25.	To what extent is there alignment between what is said **to** people and what is said **about** people?	O	P	E	U
	Right Decisions				
26.	To what extent is there alignment between leadership belief #2 (decisions made at the appropriate level) and actual practice?	O	P	E	U
27.	To what extent is there alignment between the concept of "those impacted by the decision should be involved in the decision" and actual practice?	O	P	E	U
28.	To what extent is there alignment between the trust vested in people and their demonstrated trustworthiness?	O	P	E	U
29.	To what extent is there alignment between leaders' styles and skills and the practice of decisions being made at the appropriate level?	O	P	E	U
30.	To what extent is authority for decision-making commensurate with responsibility?	O	P	E	U
	Right Consequences				
31.	To what extent is there alignment between the compensation system and the demonstrated performance of people?	O	P	E	U
32.	To what extent are benefits aligned with actual needs of people? (For example, is the benefit plan flexible enough to accommodate individual needs?)	O	P	E	U

33.	To what extent is there alignment between the criteria for advancement and demonstrated job performance? (For example, is movement to a higher role viewed as the result of competency or a reassignment based upon marginal success?)	O	P	E	U
34.	To what extent is there alignment between the quality of performance and performance evaluation data?	O	P	E	U
35.	To what extent is there alignment between the evaluation data and recognition for effectiveness?	O	P	E	U
36.	To what extent is there alignment between the evaluation data and consequences for poor performance?	O	P	E	U
37.	To what extent is there alignment between the evaluation data and the staff development component?	O	P	E	U
38.	To what extent is there alignment between student progress reporting and our mission, vision, and values?	O	P	E	U

APPENDIX B

LEADERSHIP BELIEF STATEMENTS

1. We believe all decisions should be consistent with our mission and goals, should be data based, should be anchored in sound theory and practice, and should be focused on what is best for the short and long term interests of all students.

2. We believe all decisions should be made at the most appropriate level in the organization and should be as close to the point of implementation as possible. The competency and commitment levels of those involved will help determine the appropriate level.

3. We believe our behavior should promote and encourage empowerment throughout our organization. Empowerment should be highly individualized and be a function of their development on the maturity continuum within the context of Belief Statement #1.

4. We believe we have an obligation to establish and maintain cohesive interdependent teams that have a high commitment to the organization's mission and goals.

5. We believe our behavior should promote and encourage professional autonomy and growth from independence to interdependence for individuals and teams throughout the organization.

6. We believe that we have an obligation to build in quality control and quality assurance strategies throughout the organization. Building feedback loops into the system will assist leaders in aligning mission, strategies, structures, and systems to ensure quality control and assurance throughout the organization.

LEADERSHIP BELIEF STATEMENTS

1. We believe all decisions should be consistent with our mission and goals, should be data based, should be anchored in sound theory and practice, and should be focused on what is best for the short and long term interests of all students.

2. We believe all decisions should be made at the most appropriate level in the organization and should be as close to the point of implementation as possible. The competency and commitment levels of those involved will help determine the appropriate level.

   As leaders build the capacity of their organizations, the preference and frequency of use for these decision-making strategies should be in the following order: ambassador, delegator, facilitator, mediator, negotiator, and arbitrator.

   a. When individuals and teams have the competencies and commitment to function interdependently with other teams and the system as a whole, the leader should fulfill the role of ambassador.

   b. When individuals and teams have the competencies and commitment to function independently as a team, the leader should delegate the task to a team leader or team. If the task has implications for other teams, the leader should encourage them to think interdependently.

   c. When members are competent but insecure or uncommitted to make the decision without support, the leader should assist the individual or teams by serving as a facilitator or mediator.

   d. When members lack the competence but are committed to helping make the decision, the leader needs to serve as a negotiator and help forge a satisfactory compromise.

   e. When members do not have the requisite knowledge, skills, or motivation, the leader should serve as an arbitrator and make the decision.

   When leaders believe a decision may have "fallen outside the parameters" described in Leadership Belief #1, they have an obligation to.

   ➤ approach the issue from a win/win perspective,

   ➤ help the individual or individuals understand why they believe the decision is not within the existing parameters, and

   ➤ if appropriate help the individual(s) involved to modify or reverse the decision in such a way that their integrity is enhanced rather than diminished.

167

3. We believe our behavior should promote and encourage empowerment throughout our organization. Empowerment should be highly individualized and be a function of their development on the maturity continuum within the context of Belief Statement #1. Over time, our preference and frequency of these power tools should be in the following order: legacy, referent, expert, information, reward, connective, and coercive.

4. We believe we have an obligation to establish and maintain cohesive interdependent teams that have a high commitment to the organization's mission and goals. Teams will assume leadership responsibility for identifying, achieving, and monitoring the highest standards of performance consistent with student and other stakeholder needs by capitalizing on the strength and diversity of team members and other interdependent teams. Therefore, in order to improve cohesiveness leaders should:

   a. In **Stage 1 (Testing),** design strategies that provide a safe, secure environment for team members.

   b. In **Stage 2 (Infighting**), help members view differences of opinion and disagreements as natural and healthy and to help them work through these differences. Approaching these differences from a win/win perspective rather than win/lose is imperative. These differences of opinions create opportunities for releasing the synergy within groups. This synergy should promote cooperation rather than competitiveness and should propel the group into Stage 3.

   c. In **Stage 3 (Getting Organized as a Team**), use a collaborative leadership style and help the group focus its energies on confronting issues rather than individuals, on establishing procedures for improving existing conditions, and for providing opportunities for team members to gain new knowledge and skills.

   d. In **Stage 4 (Mature Closeness as a Team),** incorporate themselves into the team as team members and leadership is truly shared. At this level of development, members of the team will feel comfortable initiating leadership acts, refocusing the group on issues, proposing improved ways of doing business, and assisting other team members in achieving quality.

   e. In **Stage 5 (Getting Organized as Interdependent Teams**), delegate the autonomy to interdependent teams and encourage them to think and act interdependently, think conceptually, search for long-term win/win strategies, provide data-based feedback, and identify needs of the team so that new skills can be developed and additional resources provided.

   f. In **Stage 6 (Mature Closeness as Interdependent Teams**), serve as ambassadors and work with other interdependent teams internal and external to the system. Members will hold themselves and others accountable for the highest standards of mission accomplishment, identify discrepancies between stakeholder needs and mission purposes, analyze causes for gaps between actual and desired results, and predict future trends and plan proactively.

5. We believe our behavior should promote and encourage professional autonomy and growth from independence to interdependence for individuals and teams throughout the organization.

   In order to encourage professional autonomy within and between teams, we believe that:

   ➤ autonomy should be highly individualized,

   ➤ autonomy should be a function of the maturity levels of individuals and teams, and

   ➤ individuals who have gained autonomy have an obligation to balance the concepts of independence and interdependence.

   When an independent decision has an impact upon another team within the organization or the unit as a whole, individuals should think "interdependence" rather than independence.

6. We believe that we have an obligation to build in quality control and quality assurance strategies throughout the organization. Building feedback loops into the system will assist leaders in aligning mission, strategies, structures, and systems to ensure quality control and assurance throughout the organization.